Henri Didon

Science Without God

Henri Didon

Science Without God

ISBN/EAN: 9783744732895

Printed in Europe, USA, Canada, Australia, Japan

Cover: Foto ©Thomas Meinert / pixelio.de

More available books at **www.hansebooks.com**

SCIENCE WITHOUT GOD

SCIENCE WITHOUT GOD

BY

H. DIDON

TRANSLATED FROM THE FRENCH BY

ROSA CORDER

"The fool hath said in his heart, There is no God"

NEW YORK
THOMAS WHITTAKER, 2 & 3, BIBLE HOUSE
1882

(All rights reserved.)

PREFACE.

No apology is needed for presenting to the English public a translation of the great Dominican's masterpiece. The evil he attacks is not confined to the Continent; and his eloquent defence of reason and humanity should be welcomed in England by every lover of truth, and by every honest doubter. The peculiar grace of the great orator's style must necessarily be somewhat lost in the translation from a Latin to a Teutonic tongue, but his scientific knowledge and fearless logic retain their force in any language. The peculiar value of these sermons, and the quality which would at once strike any one acquainted with theological writings, is that they are thoroughly of the present century, and exhibit a breadth of view and advanced scientific knowledge very seldom displayed by theologians of this or any age. Their utterly unsectarian character should commend them most especially to the consideration of the thoughtful and intelligent, for whom, as the author himself tells us, they were composed. That their influence may help to root out some of the pernicious and absurd doctrines now in vogue, and at the same time strengthen those whose faith is wavering, is the translator's very earnest hope, as it is assuredly the author's most fervent prayer.

ROSA CORDER.

CONTENTS.

INTRODUCTION.
	PAGE
FAITH AND EXPERIMENTAL SCIENCE	1

FIRST DISCOURSE.
POSITIVISM	54

SECOND DISCOURSE.
MATERIALISM	81

THIRD DISCOURSE.
ATHEISTIC PANTHEISM	105

FOURTH DISCOURSE.
SCEPTICISM	126

FIFTH DISCOURSE.
PRACTICAL ATHEISM	150

SIXTH DISCOURSE.
THE EXISTENCE OF GOD	174

SEVENTH DISCOURSE.
RATIONAL KNOWLEDGE OF GOD	196

SCIENCE WITHOUT GOD.

INTRODUCTION.

FAITH AND EXPERIMENTAL SCIENCE.

The most glorious age is that in which great questions are solved; the most stormy, that in which they are raised. It seems that on this nineteenth century the hard task has devolved of raising, without solving, the most numerous and important problems. It is now in its decline, and is still a prey to the most terrible conflicts.

The question of peace has been put forward, and has not been answered. Ten gigantic struggles of nation against nation have rendered this epoch one of the most sanguinary in history.

The social question has been put forth afresh, and has not been answered. The sinister exploits of Socialism, unchained for an instant in France, growing in America, and multiplying its threats and outrages in Germany and Russia, demonstrate this.

The question of liberty has been put forth: it has not been solved. In practice, the limits of this irresistible force have not been settled, and we are now witnessing the shameful spectacle of a pusillanimity which shrinks from carrying out to its full extent the work of enfranchisement begun by Christ, and of an inconsistent liberalism which, when in power, insolently treads underfoot the liberty it had before pretended to worship.

The political question has been raised: it has not been solved. Intellects wander at random, regardless of those laws which rule the normal development of nations. Here preachers of democracy and republicanism inveigh blindly and disdainfully against religion; as though religion was not a condition of every wise democracy and of every prosperous republic. There obstinate partisans of decayed *régimes* make of their political idea a principle as immutable as a dogma.

Our century has put forward the question of economy: it has not been solved. We have only just begun to know how to water the land that it may produce, and to diminish distances in order to facilitate commerce. The great public works of irrigation, of canal cutting, or of railroads, are abandoned, or, more often, habitually given over, to the caprices of a policy of expediency, or the unintelligent suggestions of a greedy cupidity.

The question of education has been raised: it has not been solved. The State certainly has its rights in this matter; but have not the individual and the father also theirs? People preoccupy themselves about the former—have they also thought of the latter? When by its compulsory programme the State insists upon an excessive study of Sciences, where is my guarantee? And when, to the detriment of intelligence, it falsifies and mutilates philosophic teaching, what is my defence?

The nineteenth century has put forward the religious question under many forms: it has not yet been practically solved under one. Are the relations between Church and State clearly defined in such a manner as to preserve their respective rights? Do we not every hour see armed might outrage without any consideration the holy independence of human conscience, under the most futile pretexts of national feeling, or of the pretended dogmas of a new and scientific orthodoxy? Is the question of agreement between the Church, democracy, and liberty by any means settled?

Is the most profound and, to my thinking, most urgent question of all, between modern experimental science, intoxicated by its conquests, exalted by its progress, applauded by the opinion which it governs, and religious faith retarded by its alliance with the insufficient or erroneous science of the ancients—this question, I say, so vital to those minds who desire neither to sacrifice Science or Faith, is it solved?

Everywhere are problems, everywhere strife.

The thinking few are anxious and despairing; and until in calm and in reflection reason shall have answered, passion speaks, and, instead of harmonizing all by truth and justice, it breathes everywhere a blast of hatred and discord.

In the question of peace and war, passion cries, Let us have no more war. Reason says, Let there be no more *unjust* wars. The sword which is the protection of oppressed weakness, and the safeguard of right, has a sanctity like that of the cross by which we are saved.

In the question of economy, passion cries, War to capital! Capital, affrighted, hides itself in mistrust. Reason knows neither this cry nor this mistrust. If labour has its duties, it has also its rights; and if capital has its rights, it has none the less its duties. Reason does not seek to put labour in revolt against capital, which leads only to the tyranny of the one over the other, but it endeavours to find the harmonious relation of these two necessary and indestructive forces. Then each would be appeased. The workman would know that it depended only upon himself to be a master, and the master, penetrated by the sense of his responsibility, would never forget that he is but the first of workmen. He is no longer the muscle that obeys, he has become the brain which commands; the work has not disappeared by changing its organ, it has but increased and ennobled itself.

In the question of liberty, passion, ever blind and egotistical, sees only its emancipation and forgets the curb. It thinks only of movement, but has no thought of the direction; it looks at its strength, not at the law which should guide it; or rather, it foolishly opposes force to law, action to that which directs it. It is good, certainly, to break our chains, but it is madness to tear off all restraint; and if it is necessary to exercise force, it is puerile and dangerous to leave it without guidance. Now, the restraint of liberty is authority, and its guide is the conscience. The ideal is to put in harmony these two inseparable powers, not to oppose them: to wish to exalt one to the detriment of the other leads, sooner or later, to their mutual ruin.

In the question of progress, passion and prejudice see only one side of things. We rush on to what we call advancement, without ever even asking ourselves if the object of our pursuit is more than a mirage; we forget that time must prepare and test the improvements of which we dream, and we destroy angrily and impatiently all traces of the past. Instead of inducing a fruitful evolution, we raise sterile revolutions. We blaspheme the past, instead of seeking to complete it, and, under pretext of creating a new world, accumulate a heap of ruins. I pity these ill-born sons, who are incapable of recognizing the greatness of their forefathers, and who believe with naïve arrogance that the world begins in their own heads!

Let us leave it to passion to create antagonisms, to oppose the future to the past, that which should be to that which was; and let us rather seek to reconcile the sons to their fathers: all that grows gains by the remembrance of its birth, and by drawing near to its originator.

A more liberal science of the evolution of nations would silence these senseless outcries which cause so much trouble in a country; and it would also take away all belief in these so-called Conservatives, to whom all change is a political impiety. To believe these prudent spirits, nothing is good but antiquity. The efforts of the living should be limited to its preservation or revival. Political aims, according to them, are as immutable as the genius or the temperament of a race. Ask what will be to-morrow, they will tell you, That which was yesterday. This is their one and invariable reply. It surely would be more just to answer, That which will be to-morrow is that which was not yesterday, or that which existed only in germ. Yesterday the acorn, to-day the oak.

Let us not belong to an immutable past, nor to a future without ancestry. Let us courageously prepare for what should be, remembering that to add one stone to the edifice it is necessary to know the plan, and to take into account the work of those who have laboured before us.

It is the same with regard to the teaching and education of the rising generation. Violent sectarians think only of monopolizing everything. Are they the masters? everything must at once be cast in their mould, and every growing creature be stamped with their effigy. State Reason is the mask of their tyranny. They do not come to persuade, but to compel. Instead of sending you apostles, they send you the police. Are they the vanquished? they have but one aim, to become masters in order to inflict their intolerance upon the minority.

I do not like to see truth violently forced upon any one. Why not respect each one's right, and render to the head of the family that which is of the family, to the State that which is the State's, to God that which is God's? Thus would be avoided these oppressions which disgust natures jealous of their legitimate independence; political right would be respected; and one would imitate God Himself, who fears not to leave the world to the terrible law of the struggle for existence, and to bring forth universal progress out of a pathway of blood.

Above all these questions, yet indissolubly linked with them, rises that of Religion. It is to resolve this in harmony with the intelligence of this age, without sacrificing either the rights of man or the rights of truth, that so many efforts are made. How so? say some. Is not the religious question already settled? And those troubled souls in search of a pretended solution, are they not like a disabled ship, without rudder or compass, which, instead of looking for the beacon, drifts here and there at the will of the tempest?

Certainly, if by the religious question is understood that divine Truth which is the unchangeable object of faith, or of the sovereign authority which declares it, all is solved. The creed, the gospel, and the Church are there: it is enough to open the eye and to incline the ear. But if by the religious question is meant the rational interpretation of Faith, or the harmonious alliance of the

Church with the powers of this world, at any moment of the evolution of nations, then the religious question becomes a problem, and a formidable one. It engrosses the attention, I am not afraid to assert, of the entire world, and it is being put forward clamorously in every country: in Europe and America; in the East as in the West; amongst the Slavs, the Germans, and the Anglo-Saxons, as amongst the Latin races; in Russia, the country of schism; in England and Germany, the countries of Protestantism; in Italy and Spain, where faith seemed to have kept best its outward semblance, as much as in France, where free thought is the most turbulent and aggressive.

In placing its foot upon the earth, the Church encounters political powers. How does it bear itself with regard to them? Its kingdom is not of this world, I know, but yet it must live in it. In other days it saw them at its feet, faithfully submissive, preparing it a throne and partaking with it of a sovereignty without dispute; to-day it finds them indifferent, hostile, or jealous. The problem, you see, is serious and complicated. Blind indeed are they who do not weigh its gravity and, one may add, its universality. If it exists it must be solved. To think that a Church of which Christ Himself is the corner-stone can be annihilated, is an illusion which a little history is sufficient to dissipate. And, on the other hand, how foolish to disregard the irresistible progress of human society, which makes of this world in which the Church exists, not a *terra firma*, but a moving sea!

The ship which carries Christ is divinely assisted; she sails on and can never sink, I grant, but she must have regard to current and to tempest, to accomplish her destiny and never to lose her course.

The solution cannot be attained by violence, for the simple reason that violence compromises everything and never yet solved anything. It will be the work of those guided by the light of God, and inspired by the charity of Christ; of those whose glance is sufficiently lofty and sufficiently broad to take account of every right, and to find harmony possible where others see only an irreconcilable conflict. Neither concession, nor bigotry: such must be their device. Concessions mean the abdication of a right; they are a weakness, almost an act of treason. Bigotry is persistent before impossibilities; it is the quality of a prejudiced mind, and a narrow nature carried away by passion. But between those who yield through cowardice and those who resist through stubbornness there will always be a place for those who would conciliate.

The politico-religious question whose extremes we have just indicated is assuredly one of the greatest of this century. The day in which it will be practically solved, in which the Cross shall be imposed as a peaceful check upon the swords brandished in the hands of the leaders of nations, will be one of the most splendid that has ever shone upon this earth, which, after so many centuries, drinks ever insatiably the blood of Abel. Will it ever come? Will the sons of God, and the peacemakers, as the Gospel calls them, ever have dominion over this earth, which seems a prey to violence? Why refuse all hope of this?

Man has conquered by his reason and his courage the animal kingdom; he has quelled those redoubtable mammifera who believed themselves, by their number, their strength, and their ferocity, sovereigns of this earth, which was peopled by their countless legions. Christ and His descendants will also vanquish by their divine gentleness, their charity, and their teaching, the heathen offspring of brutalized man. So much the worse for those who do not believe in good, who doubt the infinite efficacy of Christ's blood, and who impiously declare Him wanting, in that balance in which God weighs the crimes and corruption of humanity. The hierarchy is the guardian of this blood. It bears in the midst of nations and of centuries its incorruptible treasure, its sacred virtue. It is ours to make fruitful these divine powers, and to bring forth little by little, not the submission of the crown to the tiara, but, what is very different, the obedience of crowns to the conscience, which is the voice of God, and to the Gospel, which is the voice of Christ.

Above the problem of the connection between Church and State, between the hierarchy with its authority held from Christ and the changing forms of human society, going from the centuries of feudal monarchy to those of absolute monarchy, from an aristocratic government to a republic, and from a liberal republic to a democratic one—above this problem, there is one of still greater depth and importance: the problem of the connection between Reason and Faith—Faith, immovable in its dogma, like the hierarchy which is its guardian; Reason, varying according to those systems which attract it, or that opinion by which it is swayed.

Perfect harmony between Faith and Reason is a necessity for every intelligent believer. A man who believes with his mind wants to know *what* he believes, and *why* he believes. Faith does not presuppose the abdication of Reason; on the contrary, she is its divine completion, and, by accepting her testimony, man, aggrandized, raises himself to God, of whom he previously knew but the inaccessible mystery. Reason tells him that above natural humanity is God; Faith teaches him that which this ineffable God has been pleased to reveal concerning Himself.

From the days of Christ down to our own time the problem of harmony between Reason and Faith has been put and solved in a thousand ways, and from many different points of view, according to the nature of the age.

John and Paul are the first who, in the Christian era, have by divine inspiration put forward the basis of equilibrium between these two forces: Reason, whose domain is nature, man, and—if one might say so—the *exterior* of God; and Faith, whose domain is the profundity, the intimate nature, of God. The ancient Fathers and many learned and pious divines have each and all, in their centuries and in their turn, consecrated all their labour and all their genius to the solution of this great problem—the harmonious relation between Reason and Faith. Their gigantic labours are in connection with each other. All these predestined labourers, separated by centuries, sent forth by the same Spirit, continue without ever turning aside their great work of enlightenment. They bring peace to the world by enlightening it. When by their influence human reason is brought back to God in Faith, all is at peace. If the war of ideas engenders the war of men, so also does the unity of doctrines prepare the peace of nations. Now, the greatest harmony of doctrine is that which is established between Reason and Faith.

This is why the solution of this problem is so necessary: this once solved, the others are on the eve of being so; and if the others should appear to be settled, their solution would be ineffectual and useless if Faith and Reason continued to oppose each other, to misunderstand each other, and to light up an implacable war between those who believe and those who do not believe.

Under what form is the redoubtable and supreme question of the relation between Reason and Faith presented to us in this nineteenth century? Under two forms: at the opening of the century it took a rationalistic and metaphysical one; towards the end a scientific, experimental one.

Eminent philosophers, the masters of French

spiritualism, vanquishers of the sensual and material philosophy of the eighteenth century, of Condillac, Helvetius, Holbach, and La Mettrie—Cousin and Jouffroy, to name only the greatest—have always paused before Faith. Instead of rising to her height, they have drawn back in fear, looking upon her as a sublime mysticism—sublime, it is true, but still human—and persuaded that all her dogmas could be proved in a way by Reason, and by her given a rational meaning.

As a basis, rationalistic Spiritualism denied all revelation, refused to give Christ the title of God, and only saw in the Trinity a human conception of the Infinite. The Church—the hierarchy—therefore, could but be a human institution, venerable doubtless by its Founder, by its antiquity, and, above all, by the pure morality which it taught. Certainly the conflict under this aspect becomes serious; it concerns the life or the death of Faith, and of the Church as a divine institution.

Has Revelation a real existence? Have we heard God's voice? Is Christ God or man? Is the Church a supernatural work? These are the questions raised by rationalism. Believers should answer them triumphantly; and since the great rationalistic attacks of the eighteenth century, thoughtful men of the Christian Faith have often and authoritatively replied.

One cannot on these points accumulate too much light; and even after the learned treatises of both Catholic and Protestant theologians, of Pascal, of Bergier, of Du Perron, of Euler, of Jacques Abbadie, of Paley, and of countless others, there remains still a rich harvest in that new field which the eighteenth century has not explored.

We appeal to all those who have at heart the confirmation and the glory of the Christian Faith. Without doubt the problem of Faith is not a geometrical theorem, which, demonstrated by $a + b$, must convince the most stubborn mind; a moral element interposes, in the total adherence of Reason to revealed truth, which is free will, and a gift of God. But also there must be enough light, and it would be a want of respect towards God and our reason, to accept the Divine word without its having been first proved beyond all doubt that He who speaks is God. I cannot, perhaps, understand all that He says—is this surprising, since He is my Master?—but I will know that He is God; then, what more rational than to bow down before such evidence? If the object of my faith could be demonstrated, it would be on a level with my reason; and this alone would prove its inconsequence. But I prove that God places it before me, and thus Reason, by submitting, does not degrade herself; on the contrary, she becomes greater, she rises out of herself, and, guided by God, enters blindfold into the divine command.

Therein lies the whole secret of reconciling Reason and Faith in the conflict which has overturned and disorganized all minds during the first half of this century, and of which the black clouds, as on the evening of a furious battle, still obscure our sky.

This darkness must be dispersed.

As God, according to Faith, has appeared to humanity, His traces should be visible; and as the office of history is to bring to light all the phenomena of which humanity has been witness, it is fit that this science should in its advancement render a new and more solemn testimony to God, Revealed and Incarnate.

Theology has superabundantly established the expedience, the possibility, and the necessity of Divine Revelation; it is time for her to insist upon the *fact*. Historical Science now embraces every race; she has exhumed past ages as though they were contemporaries that had only yesterday been buried and disappeared. All these resuscitated epochs bear witness of God. India, China, Egypt, and the ancient races of America bear the imprint of His footstep through all ages and nations.

Let them, then, be made to speak, and may enlightened opinion in this cause pronounce a decisive verdict from its own conscience.

The conflict between contemporary Reason and Faith was not prolonged under that form beyond the first half of this century. It is a strange thing, and one which will show to what oscillations that inconstant sea called public opinion is condemned. Whilst spiritualistic rationalism reigned in France, and proclaimed with eloquence, if not with originality, those dogmas which are the honour of philosophy—the existence of God, providence, the spirituality of the soul, its immortality, and free will and a future life;—while, proud of following Plato, Augustine, and Descartes, by recalling the most flourishing ages of Greece, of Rome, and of the great century, rationalism opposed all revealed doctrine, and refused to admit a revealed God, a Christ, or a Church divinely appointed—gradually a change in opinion began to show itself.

By the side of philosophers absorbed in metaphysics appear philosophers eager for experience: the former, dazzled by the greatness of the soul, speak only of psychology; the latter, more realistic, fascinated by matter, speak of physiology. A new kind of materialism has risen up against the spiritualism of past ages. To metaphysical Science, which only concerns itself about the invisible, is opposed experimental Science, which concerns itself with the visible, with that which can be seen, weighed, and measured, and which limits itself to phenomena. And, just as rationalistic Spiritualism declared itself an enemy to Faith and revelation, experimentalism proclaims itself the determined enemy of metaphysical spiritualism.

Infatuated rationalists said, We will have no revelation above our reason; the followers of experimentalism cry, There is no metaphysic beyond our experience.

The brilliant reign of metaphysics has soon declined; the pulpits are silent, the masters have disappeared one by one, the books which perpetuated in a style worthy of a great age the ideas of antiquity are forgotten: decidedly opinion has changed.

Instead of analyzing the facts of the conscience, we analyze the facts of nature; instead of studying the soul, we study the body; spirit is neglected, and matter prevails.

We who are of this generation have been witness of this singular revolution. We have seen the heavens veil themselves, and that youth which applauded enthusiastically the noble titles of a free and spiritual soul, has given place to a positive generation which weighs everything and applauds nothing—I am wrong, it applauds matter. Absorbed by this, its soul contracts, and, while weighing the visible, loses all sense of the ideal or the infinite.

There is in this phenomenon something to disquiet the observer. Those who look beyond and foresee the future are terrified to see the wave of positivism rise.

It is not by turning over the earth that man will find his perfection; it is by endeavouring to raise himself up to God. The earth! Man is greater than it; and since what date has any one perfected himself by contact with that which is inferior? I fear to see minds thus absorbed in the visible; all that is seen is temporal, fleeting, miserable; that which is not seen is eternal.

The present generation, I fear, can but deteriorate. Speak to it of that it cannot touch, it smiles; speak to it of God and it turns away. But what, indeed, remains to man when he is limited to matter, and what is he worth when he no longer believes himself the son of God?

He turns to animalism.

And then you see him absorbed in the endeavour to bring himself to the level of the mammalia of which he is the companion, and among whom he seeks for ancestors. He applies to this work all his labour and his science. Matter is everything with him. The animal is a second self. Occasionally he yields him the palm, and while studying the bees, the ants, the beavers, he asks himself in what respect man surpasses his illustrious congenitors, from whom he may well ask for lessons.

But human nature has its laws. The great type of being has not been abandoned to the caprice of foolish creatures. God, who made all, does not will that man can at his pleasure upset everything and undo himself. Earth cannot long contain him; matter fascinates him but for an hour. He experiences a salutary reaction, and with the same energy with which he searched once into the domain of experience, he now explores the depths of the human conscience and the laws of humanity, and listens to the voice of God speaking to him from on high.

The type does not belie itself. Seek to violate it, within two or three generations it reappears. Then who will dare to say that the highest type, man, does not contain all together: the earth, since he was formed from it; spirit, since he is intelligent and free; the infinite, since nothing created can satisfy him?

Man may strive his utmost, matter, however

learnedly treated, cannot long prevail within him against his spirit and against God.

Meanwhile the struggle is a hot one, and for more than twenty years we have witnessed a conflict of a new kind between Reason and Faith. This conflict, for all who think, is the dominant fact of our age.

So long as it lasts the minds that it has shaken cannot regain their balance. We see them taking refuge in a sentimental mysticism, or wrapping themselves in a narrow positivism, or in materialism, or sleeping—one may say killing themselves—in scepticism. Those who have at heart the development of the mind, those who would by no means wish to lessen humanity, those who seek to put into harmony—in that nature in which all that is seems to be united,—matter, mind, and God—can these stand by and see perpetuated, to the detriment of our country, our civilization, and our faith, the conflict which tortures this sick generation?

Hostilities are on both sides difficult to appease. The least blunder may kindle the war, and peace often requires both genius and virtue.

Peace is urgently needed.

If one should perish, even, beneath the labour it demands, no hesitation is possible; we cannot purchase it at too high a price. The world fights in the name of experimental Science, and in the name of Faith. We do not wish a truce; we seek for a lasting peace.

Is it possible?

Let us first seek to know the two sides; we shall find out afterwards, perhaps, the secret of pacifying them.

Faith, for well-nigh twenty centuries, has ruled the world, repeating by the mouth of her ministers, commissioned by Christ, the same creed, making every intelligence read in the same inspired Book the same eternal dogmas.

Before her to-day, scientific reason haughtily opposes itself.

I name thus that reason which by observation and experience has studied nature, has noted the connection of phenomena, the conditions of life and thought; that reason which knows that worlds are born, grow, and die; that reason which has read in the past the history of the earth, and which foresees its dark future and its death.

Last outcome of the culture and development of man, experimental Science believes itself the very highest of all powers. Like the so-called "self-made man," it disdains all that is not itself. Not content with disdaining metaphysics and religion, it dares to suppress them both, as incapable of leading us to the truth.

Nothing is true, says positive Science superbly, but that which is subject to the control of experience: but neither the object of metaphysics nor the object of religion can be so controlled; therefore neither the systems of religion nor the systems of metaphysics can be discussed. Mere questions of sentiment, they have nothing absolute, nothing scientific. Objections may be raised against them, but they will not entertain them.

And it puts forth this fatal dilemma: no middle course; either see or believe—either see by science, or believe by faith. It is impossible, without inconsequence or weakness, to be both a scientific man and a believer. Whoever wishes to be the disciple of science must say adieu for ever to the simple beliefs of religion. The laboratory is from henceforth his temple; the phenomena of nature his Bible; the struggle for existence his code; matter his God.

In the presence of experimentalism, become under our very eyes a system of encroachment which would suppress all that experience does not verify, philosophy and religion have but one attitude possible. There is one harmony to seek for; contradictions can never agree; war is declared. Either positivism or Faith and metaphysics must succumb.

An eminent philosopher fancied he had discovered the secret of agreement between Science exclusively experimental, and metaphysics; he only succeeded in sacrificing the latter by taking from the conceptions which are its sublimity all objective value. If by the opposition of Science and Faith is meant the violent opposition of positivism and religion, to look for agreement is futile, to hope for harmony useless.

The dilemma is forced upon us—either to see or to believe.

But without here pausing to refute positivism, I would only ask, Is it identical with experimental Science? If it was proved that, according to the dogma of positivism, Science is everything, it must be proved that metaphysics are useless and faith an illusion. Has Science proved this? No.

Then in what name do you forbid me to explore in an appropriate manner a region which is closed to Science? Science has one domain, Faith has another; by what right, I repeat, does positivism forbid me access to it? Experimental Science cannot enter it, I know; but is experimenting the only end of man? I touch the phenomenon, but I conclude the invisible cause from it; I see the phenomenon, but I affirm strictly and logically, without seeing it, the cause. Where is the contradiction? Why should Science take exception to matters beyond its province. In the same way with regard to Reason and Faith. Reason proves, Faith accepts, a divine testimony. Where is the opposition? An intelligent being and capable of knowing, have I not an equal right to demonstrate that which I know, and to accept on those grounds the testimony of a mind superior to myself? When I demonstrate I perform an act of logical reason; when I bow to divine testimony I perform both an act of logic, as I bow only before a proof, and an act of faith, as I accept a testimony. Where is the contradiction?

Experience has but one right over metaphysics, that of forbidding them to suppose causes which are contradicted by the phenomena; and metaphysics has but one over faith—that is, to oblige it to prove its title, and never to bow before false evidence. Science, which exacts more, oversteps its legitimate limits; that reason which would go further belies itself. The divers movements of experimental, logical, and religious reason are not at war; they follow different roads and different levels: they compete, but cannot contradict each other. Positivism may affirm to the contrary; assertions are easy to make, let it essay to prove them.

Experimental Science has not been monopolised by positivism.

Most minds have understood that phenomena, in spite of the attraction of their testimony, the harmony of their succession, the certainty of their connection, do not satisfy our longing to *know*. Positivism may think what it likes, its doctrines will not prevent human intelligence from being what it is. Now, intelligence is so constituted that behind the *Effect* it looks for the *Cause*, and, in the multiplicity of phenomena, the Unity from which they are derived. An imperious force, which it cannot escape, pushes it through all to the First Cause, without which nothing can be explained. In spite of the contempt, the abuse, and the prophecies of positivism, metaphysics remain and force themselves upon our minds. Of what service are these metaphysics, if not to be raised by reason to those causes unattained by experience, and to determine, with a certainty in no way inferior to that of experimental Science, the First Principle, the Sovereign Law, the Supreme End of being.

Also, in this century so in love with positive Science, in this generation given over unrestrainedly to the worship of mathematics, disdaining all which is not numbered, or weighed, or to be touched, the greater part of the savants, chemists or physicians, physiologists or astronomers, anthropologists or therapeutists, all the while protesting with the positivists their scepticism in metaphysics and their sovereign worship of exact and experimental sciences, none the less have a system of metaphysics of their own. They make one, it might be said with all due respect, as Molière's hero made prose, without knowing it.

If at least guarded against the vertigo of Science, they would only raise a correct system of philosophy without violating the first laws of reason and logic; but, absorbed by that visible universe of which they study the innumerable and remarkable manifestations, they become incapable of raising themselves to the transcendent Cause. They vegetate in atheism; the grandeur of the work, better known by a more advanced Science, makes them misconceive the Workman. They glorify nature, and, to the disregard of the fundamental principles of reason, falsify or suppress God.

As they admit the search for a first cause, they ought to say, "The universe, as proved by experimental Science, is on the system of a progressive evolution, from brute matter up to thought itself.

Who produces this evolution?" Logically, and according to the principle of causality, they should reply, An intelligent cause, transcending the universe, and Infinite. Intelligent; for if it had no power of thought, how would thought have existed? Transcendent—in other words, *exceeding* and *containing* the world it has produced, as, if it did not exceed, how could it *contain*, and if it could not contain, how could it *produce* the world? Infinite; for Infinitude alone can explain an indefinite evolution such as is shown in human thought.

Instead of resolving in this way the problem of the First Cause, which is the central point of all metaphysics, the majority of savants fall into two capital errors.

Some, struck with the prominent part played by matter in all phenomena, seeing that thought, even, is never without a material substance, observing that everything begins with matter; having sophistically confounded the point of departure with the effective principle, and the *conditions* of a fact with its *cause*—the materialists have said, All is matter. All comes from matter; in it all ends, by it all moves. It is the beginning, the middle, and the end. The spirit (or mind) is but a word, a property of matter; it is only to be conceived on these conditions. Eternal, indestructible, at bottom always the same, matter is the only substance of which phenomena of all kinds are but the ephemeral and mobile manifestations.

Others of greater imagination, less fascinated by matter, captivated more by a vague notion of force, which defines nothing and lends itself easily to all, incapable, like the first, of raising themselves above the universe to a transcendent Cause, disliking at the same time to make, with the materialists, matter the cause of mind—the pantheists, to call them by their name, have imagined the universe to be a single being, animated by one force, and which goes on developing itself alone from nothing up to everything, in space without limit, and time without end. It is the eternal *to be*.

Materialism sacrifices the first principle of reason by making matter the cause of thought; naturalistic pantheism suppresses it, by affirming that the progressive universe *makes itself!*

Such is, in a few words, the state of public reason. Scepticism, positivism, materialism, pantheism, atheism—these different systems weigh down experimental Science under a disastrous yoke, and must be hailed as the first cause of this fierce conflict between Reason and Faith.

The first work of whoever wishes to reconcile them should be to distinguish, at the outset, experimental Science from those philosophic doctrines which have more or less perverted it, and which, by false interpretations, have put it in antagonism with Faith.

We have attempted this preliminary labour. The sermons we have published under the significant title of "Science without God," have for their only object the exposure and summary refutation of those systems which, explicitly or not, pretend to confiscate experimental Science to their exclusive profit, and to make it an irreconcilable enemy to all religion, and a servant of atheism and materialism. And though one may be little able to cast aside preconceived ideas, and be re-instructed on the nature of positive Science, it is not so difficult to clear Science, and to free her from all bondage.

The reader will judge if we have succeeded.

Materialism and pantheism, no less than positivism, have nothing in common with experimental Science.

They are both metaphysical systems, ways of replying to that problem of a First Cause which torments every mind, and on which positivism in vain seeks to impose silence. On the other hand, experimental Science is the direct and sensible knowledge of phenomena and their experimental conditions—no matter what may be the idea held concerning the Cause from which they are derived.

For those who confound by prejudice, like Doctors Büchner and Haeckel, Science with materialism, the antagonism between Faith and Science is absolute. To wish to harmonize them is to wish an impossibility; between materialism which denies the soul, pantheism which denies God, and faith which affirms both God and the soul, all compromise is absurd. But upon what grounds can the partisans of atheistic Science go, in order to confound experimental Science with materialism and pantheism? Such confusion is arbitrary, illogical, and impious. And yet, is it credible that minds otherwise farsighted cannot see that experimental Science is the same to the atheist and to the believer, to the materialist and the spiritualist, to the positivist and to the pantheist? Experimental Science does not change with the metaphysical doctrines of those who cultivate it; therefore it is distinct from them. The argument is unanswerable. I content myself with it for the time being; and I beg all those scientific men who pose as materialists, pantheists, or atheists, to be kind enough to show me in what respect experimental Science gives them the least cause for so doing.

The discourses that we here publish prove, on the contrary, how Science, interpreted by a reason which respects its own laws, leads all earnest minds to God, and how, in order to force Science into giving evidence in favour of materialism or atheism, reason becomes unjust to herself, commits as it were suicide, treads under her feet all logic, and surrenders herself to the grossest sophisms.

It is time to publish before the world these capital offences against reason daily committed by men whose science is incontestable, and who for that reason exercise a real influence over the public mind. We must not suffer their scientific value to blind us to their bad philosophy, nor allow them to become, by reason of that science, professors of atheism and materialism. We are ready to do every one justice, but we are also determined to unmask these false pretences. We ask no better than to salute in the man of science the complete master: is it our fault if experience has absorbed the mind, and if the great faculties of reason have become deadened? The human mind is both earthly and divine. The earthly part is magnificent: is it our fault if the divine has disappeared? May it please God that they give back to this generation the wings they have shorn from it, and that we may see once more revive intellects of height, of breadth, and of depth sufficient acutely to discern the phenomena of the earth, thoughtfully to sound the most secret depths of the soul, and open to all that is truth, to receive the revelations of Faith?

Our dearest ambition is to work for this end. We believe ourselves to be serving this great cause by breaking the tyranny which to-day has made Science into a mere slave. I plead here for liberty. Science is captive: let her be delivered! She stifles under the weight of a dogmatism without logic or greatness: let her be suffered to breathe.

To make free is to make sound. Let us, then, free Science.

Truly this peaceful crusade is worth more than the others.

If the Holy Land, seven centuries ago, was in the power of the sons of Mahomet, the Spirit of Christ at least was free, and ran in the veins of twenty new races. Experimental Science is part of the

Word of God. This Word is captive in a sepulchre guarded by the false systems of a philosophy without God. Let us break open this sepulchre of captivity; open the crusade in favour of the light-giving captive; and oppose to a fettered Science a free Science, which has nothing to fear from Faith, any more than Faith has to fear from her.

Given its independence, does experimental Science remain in conflict with Faith? To believe certain scientific men, such conflict is unavoidable.

I admit that I cannot comprehend such an opinion, and before showing the falseness of the grounds upon which it is founded, I wish to prove that between Science freed from false systems, and metaphysical faith, separated from all human alloy, the conflict cannot exist.

After all, what is antagonism? The encounter of two forces advancing on the same ground in opposite directions. Two forces are not on the same ground, and their encounter, and consequently their shock, is rendered impossible. They are on the same ground, but, instead of being in opposition, they are parallel or divergent; their encounter and shock is again impossible. Let experimental Science and Faith represent two forces, and for them to be in conflict with each other it is necessary that they should operate in different directions on the same given ground.

If experimental Science and Faith are studied from this point of view, they will be found to differ in their *object* or *ground*, in their *method* or *direction*, and consequently in their aim.

The *object* of experimental Science is the visible and material phenomenon—that which is evident to the senses, and can be seen, touched, weighed, and measured. She seeks for the order of phenomena, and determines anterior phenomena according to those conditions which govern the subsequent phenomena. Her *method* is bringing intelligence to bear upon the facts of nature by experience and observation. Nothing in Science is certain but what has been experienced and observed. Facts alone are her concern. Hypothesis has no definite value until it has been directly verified. Until then it is merely provisional; its justness and stability are in proportion to the number of facts it serves to explain. Theories depend upon the hypothesis upon which they are founded. The true savant is ever ready to abandon his theories when facts contradict them, and to reject an hypothesis whenever a new fact appears in opposition to it. Hypotheses are mere guesses of man's mind, often deceitful, like him, and like him always diffident. Theories represent human wisdom, often at fault, always in some direction insufficient; facts alone are immutable, for they express the will and the thought of God, who neither lies nor changes.

The triumph of experimental genius is to seize the limited connection between certain facts, and to group them according to truth. The higher the genius, the more numerous the facts to which its vast synthesis will apply; but, however strong its wing, it is soon tired, and cannot attain the inaccessible height from whence in time and space the universality of phenomena spreads before its eyes.

Know and *do*—these words sum up the aim and end of Science. Let us understand them. Know what? Do what? Know the order of sensible phenomena and the condition by which they are manifested and determined, and command matter. Science confers on man the mastership of the universe; he becomes through her the lieutenant of God. Like Him he can say, Let there be light, and there is light; Let there be life, and there is life. God has but to will and to command, and nature obeys Him. Man has but to put the conditions established by God, and matter obeys him.

From this point of view who would not be fascinated by the greatness and the power of Science? Is it nothing to subdue matter, to enchain it, to hold thunder and fire in your hand, to annihilate and transform a world at your will? Man is none the less great although fixed upon this narrow globe, where he is held by a force which only death can break, but, king of the earth, proves by this very science that the whole universe is his domain.

The object, the method, and the aim of Science thus determined, it will be easy to see whether its conflict with Faith is possible.

What is the object of Faith? The phenomenon? No. The First Principle, the Absolute Cause, God. The phenomenon is on an inferior ground, for every principle and cause is superior to the phenomena which it produces. The phenomenon is contained *by* them; *it* does not contain them.

Thus God can be observed in two ways: as He is manifested by the phenomena of the universe of nature and humanity, and as He surpasses everything visible; in a word, in His transcendence and His very Being. From this point of view is He the precise object of Faith.

What is God in Himself? God alone knows. What is His will concerning His creation? God alone knows. Has He revealed it to man? This all intelligent Christians must prove *rationally* by irrefutable signs.

The mystery of the inner life of God, the immediate connection of the divine and human nature in Christ, the direct and voluntary connection of human nature with the divine essence by the intermediation of Christ—this is in three words the *object* of Faith, of which the divine Word contains the only revelation. In what respect, may I ask, do the phenomena of nature and humanity which engross the attention of Science, place themselves in opposition to divine faith? One speaks of the phenomena of the universe, the other of the transcendent Principle of the universe. The objects are distinct, the grounds superposed; therefore the forces moving on these superposed grounds cannot encounter each other.

The same truth is evident when the *method* of Faith is inquired into.

The whole process of Faith consists in this: to adhere to the testimony of God, who is never

D

deceived, as He is infinitely wise, and who never deceives, as He is goodness and uprightness itself. Science interrogates nature: nature replies by facts. Faith interrogates God: God answers by revealing what He is. He testifies His presence by signs not contained in nature, as they are departures from its laws, and prove God's intervention, as God alone could have been the cause.

I have described miracle and prophecy.

Christ rose from the dead—here is a miracle. Christ predicted His resurrection—here is a prophecy. The miraculous event is not in the laws of nature; it oversteps them. Prophecy is not the law of humanity; the future is veiled to man. But both become God, who is the Master of nature and can therefore modify it; who is the Eternal Present, and therefore knows the Future.

Between the method of Science and that of Faith where is the conflict? They differ, as do the objects to which they correspond, but they are no more opposed than the two domains contradict each other.

There remains the aim or end of Faith.

What is it?

To conduct humanity to its ideal perfection, to its absolute end; to reunite men of good inclinations, by the intercession of Christ the revealer and Saviour, to that God who has created them, who calls them, and who waits for them.

See, then, the difference and the harmonious contrast between Science and Faith: one is terrestrial, the other celestial; the one makes us look on the earth where all is passing, the other to heaven where there is rest; one is limited to teaching us the phenomena which disappear before our eyes, the other rises to the inaccessible Substance which never changes; one gives us a planet for our domain, the other promises us the kingdom of God; one exalts our animality, the other deifies us by enfranchisement; one leaves us in the matter from which we were formed, the other revives us by the Spirit which has breathed upon us: the one makes us, as Claud Bernard said, the foremen of nature; the other, as Saint John said, the adopted sons of God.

Where is the opposition? Let the wise ones tell us. I see in these two destinies but a harmonious contrast. Science and Faith do not exclude each other, any more than does the earth, heaven; or matter, mind. These things should not oppose each other, but become united; their accord is the greatest marvel and *chef-d'œuvre* of creation.

And yet the conflict exists. Noisy and vindictive, it fills with the sound of its hate this land, this age, and the civilized world; and of all the wars which have stirred up mankind there is none more obstinate. I would be the last to deny this sad fact; I have noticed it with emotion, even in these very pages, and I deplore it. But I simply conclude that, without doubt, either the men of Science or the men of Faith, perhaps both, are in the wrong, and that their warfare is impious and absurd.

The colours they bear were meant to mingle their folds, not to destroy each other; the causes they serve should not oppose or crush each other, but be joined together and triumph by their union.

History is full of these saddening facts—result of the ignorance, narrow-mindedness, prejudices, and passions of men. That the conflict may cease it is necessary to discover the culprits. Where are they? To which side do they belong? They are amongst the learned and amongst the believers. I say it simply and frankly, may I have the pardon of both. My intention is not either to slight the servants of Science nor the servants of Faith; a devoted and, I may say, passionate friend of both Science and Faith, my only aim is, by studying the causes which put them in opposition, to serve and fortify both, by bringing together in peace and truth those men who master the earth, and those men who by faith would conquer heaven.

The first and greatest wrong committed by men of Science is to mix up metaphysical doctrines with Science, and cleverly invest the one with the authority of the other.

It would be easy for me to quote names in support of my assertion, and to show, proof in hand, materialism—*monism* as the modern pantheists call it—inspiring many a work of popular Science. The Germans are particularly distinguished in this confusion; Büchner and Haeckel —the one an apostle of extreme *monism*, and the other the apologist of the most declared materialism —are the most salient types of this mania for sheltering under the cloak of an "advanced Science" doctrines which have nothing whatever in common with it.

They enslave and falsify Science, and do not even prove the theory that they extol. When they have affirmed that the universe is in course of evolution—which is an indisputable scientific fact—have they also established the theory that this evolution has no *cause*, and that, therefore, monism is the sole new conception with regard to the origin of being authorized by Science? Why, then, these gratuitous assumptions? They can only seduce weak minds or impress the young. Not content with confiscating to their profit Science itself, these false savants, wrapped up in their own metaphysics, pervert the reason of their disciples, and arouse not only the passions, but, worse still, the intellect, against that faith which, without flinching, preserves the ancient and healthy doctrine of a God transcending the universe, the cause, law, and end of its progress.

Such conduct is perfidious. It can only commend itself to sectarians; and it is more than time that we should see rise up against it the protest of every free and upright soul, and of every disinterested man of Science.

Another fault of scientific men is, on the one hand, an almost total ignorance of the Faith they attack; on the other, the misconception of the elements which constitute Science.

For to know, if two things are harmonious or

contradictory, in what respect they agree or in what they are opposed, it is necessary to know both with *exactitude*, and in no way to confound their various elements. Thus, whoever takes as a set form of Faith the more or less exact interpretations of it given by men, proves by that that he is ignorant of its very essence; and whoever presents as indisputable facts the hypotheses or theories of Science, proves by that that he is wanting in scientific discernment.

Faith, be it known, comprises four distinct elements: the formula, or exact enunciation of the truth to be believed; example: There are three persons and one God. The interpretation sanctioned by the authority and decision of the Church; example: Christ's presence in the Holy Eucharist. The interpretation which, without this supreme guarantee, rests upon the unchangeable truths of philosophy, and forms the great tradition of the philosophic and theological teaching of the Doctors; example: the established principles of the Incarnation. Lastly, the interpretation resting upon contestable philosophic opinions, or upon an incomplete and erroneous Science; example: the scientific explanation of Genesis by the Ptolemaic system, or of the resurrection by the physiology of Galen.

On the other hand, it is necessary to distinguish in Science, *facts, hypotheses, and theories.* Facts well proved are undeniable; example: no life without organic matter placed under the appropriate conditions of air, heat, and moisture. Hypotheses are provisionary—uncertain until directly verified; example: the existence of an imponderable body, ether. Theories are disputable; example: light is the vibration of ether under the solar influence.

These principles being stated, it is easy to see that the man of Science who is ignorant of Faith, or who confounds the elements of his Science, may create a thousand conflicts; but such antagonisms are vain and imaginary, and only serve to prove one thing—the ignorance, shallowness, or prejudice of the man of Science.

For a conflict to exist between Science and Faith with any reason, it will be necessary to bring forward one legitimately controllable and irrefutable scientific fact, which contradicts a single dogma or interpretation sanctioned by the Church, or a single rationally certain truth. But we say aloud, Such a fact does not exist; and we add fearlessly, If it does, show it us!

All the contradictions of which certain men of Science have made so much, and which a certain American author has collected under the title of "The Conflict of Science and Religion," merely rest upon ignorance of the Faith, or the confusion of the divers elements of Science.

They say, Faith teaches that the earth is the centre of the universe, and man the centre of creation; Science has proved the contrary; hence contradiction. I reply, Faith does not teach what you say it does. You take as a dogma that which was at one time an interpretation of a dogma, according to an imperfect astronomy and anthropology;

hence the contradiction is but apparent. They say again, Faith teaches that the world is governed by the providence of a personal God; Science has proved the contrary; hence contradiction. I reply, How has Science proved this? She shows us one invariable order in all phenomena, but has she established that this order is not the expression of the wisdom and the will of a personal God, and that in certain cases it cannot be supplanted by the free intervention of an absolute Force?

A Science which supported such a theory would not be true; she would be out of her province; she would deceive. Thus, it is the glory of Faith to be at war with *false* Science, and the wrong here is on the side of the savants, who, to contradict God, tread underfoot both logic and reason.

Voltaire believed himself to triumph against Faith, when, in the name of the then prevalent theory which regarded the sun as the sole source of light, he taxed the Bible with absurdity. The Bible teaches, said he, that light was created before the sun; this is absurd, as it has been *demonstrated* that the sun produces light. Voltaire confounded in his Science *Theory* and *Fact*. If he had remembered that Theory is fallible, he would have respected what he too lightly ridiculed. There may be scientific theories in opposition with Faith: for a believer this proves their falseness; for a savant who does not believe, it should be a sign to make him reflect; and if he is wise he should pause before concluding against Faith, unless he wishes to imitate the simplicity of Voltaire.

These examples are sufficient to demonstrate the inanity, the bad logic, and in every case the hidden cause, of these conflicts between Science and Faith. We could enumerate them one by one; all, without exception, rest on one or other of the motives we have attempted to bring to light. We leave this easy task to the reader; he knows the field to be reaped from, let him gather his own harvest.

If the learned, more or less hostile to Faith, are the principal cause of the strife we deplore, those who side with Faith, who defend it, if not with ability, at least valiantly—the believers,—let us not fear to say it—are not entirely without reproach. There would be both blindness and disloyalty in the attempt to deny it.

We are not of those who practise the miserable maxim, "It's true, but you mustn't say it." Dissimulation has never served but to lose the best of causes; if it ever gained one, it was not with honour.

If men of Science live often in a systematic ignorance of the teaching of Faith, and if before combating her they content themselves often with a merely superficial knowledge, the men who to-day profess religious Science are not always themselves sufficiently instructed in natural and experimental Science.

What! they will say, supposing Faith to be exact, can one make it a grievance that those men who profess divine Science should ignore terrestrial Science? This domain is unworthy of them; it is not proper that minds open to the contemplation of divine mysteries should be implicated in the profane labour of the study of created things.

To reply to these too disdainful doctors, lost in their own sublimity, I could limit myself to invoking the testimony—an irrefutable one, this—of Thomas Aquinas, the greatest of doctors and the most complete of masters. Let them open the "Summa contra Gentiles," and let them learn in the school of this genius, whose greatness knew how to contain and harmonize all the known truths of his age, in what manner the theologian should study nature, and how it can be of use to him. Such testimony would satisfy those who like to take refuge under the shelter of a great name; at the same time, I wish to insist upon this capital point, and reply to the objection by penetrating the very heart of the difficulty.

People are mistaken about the true nature of Theology. Theology is not Faith; it is the *science* of Faith. Faith is necessary to every Christian; Theology is not. Faith makes believers; Theology, those learned or *docte* in the Faith. What is necessary to the science of Faith? I reply, It is necessary to apply all human knowledge to the understanding of the mysteries of God. Theological Science comprehends, in the first place, revealed truths, with all the conclusions and all the suggestions that a logical reason can set forth and deduce; in the second place, all those rational explanations which, founded upon philosophy and experimental Science, show forth the established truths of our dogmas, and their close harmony with the laws of nature and the principles of reason. Thus, is it not by the philosophic study of the soul that we perceive the ineffable mystery of the Trinity? And the experimental sciences, geology, anthropology, and physiology, are they not necessary conditions of the explanation—always wanting, certainly, as it is human, but still most useful—of the formation of the world, the creation of man, the resurrection, and many other mysteries?

Science, you see, forms an *integral part* of universal Theology. Without it one may be a casuistical Theologian—one in the limited sense of the word; one is not *the* Theologian.

The type of the savant in Faith is Thomas Aquinas. The most famous monument of scientific Faith is the "Summa Theologica" and the "Summa contra Gentiles." All the light brought by divine revelation into the world, the philosophy of incontestable truths, natural Science, whether of language, discovery, or experience—all are condensed in the masterly works of this great genius.

He was predestined by Providence, who gave him for ancestors, amongst the dead, Aristotle and Augustine; for father and for master, amongst the living, that great intelligence, who knew how to unite with revealed and philosophic Science all the experimental Science of his age—I mean Albertus Magnus. It is too often forgotten that Thomas Aquinas had as guide this tremendous man; and that the Archbishop of Cologne, the great Dominican, was the most universal genius of his age, and that all natural Science was interpreted by him.

If we wish to revive Theology in its entirety, we must teach young believers every human Science, and if we wish to resuscitate Thomas Aquinas, we must first evoke Albertus Magnus.

Study the *Summa* of the master; examine it carefully from the treatise on the existence of God down to the last conclusion; not a question, not an article in which natural Science does not bear witness to Faith, and enter, as an integral part, into the universal synthesis.

Theology is most particularly *the* universal and synthetical Science. In it scientific, philosophic, and revealed truths harmonize, and from all these united rays the knowledge of God shines forth more luminously. Well! since the work is done, what more can we want? The Theological monument is raised; let it lie down in its shadow without heeding the unquiet wave of human thought. God forbid that I should undervalue the finished and immortal work of Thomas Aquinas! The spirit is ever the same, and ever living; but the letter waxes old and dies. The theological spirit, of which the Angelic Doctor was, perhaps, the most powerful incarnation, cannot change; but its creations must, and indeed should, alter. The placing all experimental and philosophic Science in harmony with revelation is the true spirit of Theology. It cannot die out without detriment to the generation and the race that suffers its decline; but that this harmony should be established between such and such a prevailing Science in some one age or country, and Faith, ever unchangeable throughout all ages and races —this is the work susceptible of opportune modifications.

The natural Science, the physics, the astronomy, and the physiology of the ancients no longer exist; proved to be either false or ignorant, they cannot serve as human explanations of the truths of Faith. The analogies that one would draw from them would neither be solid in themselves, nor would they possess any power over the minds of the intelligent.

What must be done, then?

The conclusion is obvious and inevitable: we must make ourselves masters of modern experimental Science, whose progress and whose discoveries are incontestable, and we must use it to the honour of the Faith, just as Saint Thomas Aquinas himself, thanks to his synthetic method, knew how to make use of the natural Science of his master, Albertus Magnus.

Those who are anxious for the triumph of Faith have no illusions to cherish and no time to lose. Science is growing; she becomes in the eyes of many an authority from which there is no appeal. Certain minds disdain her: let them take care; disdain is easy, but victory is less so. It is not sufficient to despise in order to conquer. Truth can be served by other means.

If we do not apply ourselves earnestly to the conquest of the natural sciences, the fatal result is to be foreseen; we shall lose, little by little, the ascendency which masters of the Faith exercise over the public mind. Respect and prestige are the necessary aureole of those who wish to be obeyed. More, not only do believers deprive themselves of a grand testimony in favour of their Faith, and of evidence which flatters peculiarly this generation enamoured of positive Science, but they prepare themselves terrible enemies. Science prosecuted without them and outside them will be turned against them; the amphitheatres and laboratories will become arsenals, where will be forged arms perfected to combat them. I am uneasy about any power which does not belong to me and which is not on my side; for the enemy may seize upon it, and if he confiscates it to his advantage, what is to prevent his turning it against me?

Nevertheless, is not this what is going on under our very eyes?

Experimental Science extends her conquests; but to whose advantage? Her own doubtless, and God's, who is the Master of every Science; but also to that of all who have had the ability and the activity, the intelligence and the perseverance, to conquer her. Free thought is everywhere in Science: it is in astronomy, in chemistry, in biology, in sociology, in anthropology; there is not one of those sciences that has not been seized upon and made to lie against God, against Christ, and against the soul.

Let others feel tranquil; for our own parts, we cannot help being both impatient and ardent. Let others feel secure about the very shafts which strike them from every side; for our own parts, we would rather of these despised arrows make an offensive weapon.

Truly the temple is solid, for it rests upon that corner-stone which is Christ—is that any reason for allowing it to be invested? That it will not be destroyed is my conviction; but neither should it be left amongst men without respect and without honour. Its light is the eternal flame of God; why should we not also illumine it with every earthly splendour? Science holds the secrets of such illumination, but only unfolds them to energetic minds.

Meanwhile—God forbid that I should forget it!—many believers have resolutely devoted themselves to gleaning in the immense and ever-extending field of experimental Science.

The clergy themselves—at least, a certain number—both in France and elsewhere, do not fear to put their hand boldly to the pickaxe which digs into the unexplored world of Science. And it is not one of the least honours of the French clergy that they see one of their representatives in almost every corner of the domain of Science—geology, archæology, anthropology, physics and chemistry, astronomy, natural history, and physiology. It is a good augury. Thanks to the work of these specialists, general ideas of Science are gradually spreading amongst us. Instead of being always on the defensive to refute, by arguments that our adversaries can challenge, the sophisms of a warped Science, we shall on our side take the offensive; and without troubling ourselves about the antagonisms which the materialists, the pantheists, or the positivists of Science affect to multiply, we shall establish harmony between Experience, Reason, and Faith. From thenceforward Science, now an obstacle to the turning of minds towards Christian dogmas, will become a new road towards them, and I seem already to see our youth following in this path of light which leads to the temple of which Christ is God.

Is it not Buffon, the great naturalist, who says, "The truths of nature will be discovered only with time, and the sovereign Master reserves them as the surest means of calling men to Himself, when faith, declining with the course of ages, becomes vacillating"?

There is yet one peril into which imprudent apologists would drag us.

Let us not be carried away by the reigning Theories of Science; they have their day. Let us use them as we would use arms, ready to lay them down when a more complete Science breaks them in our hands. When we interpret a dogma or a revealed book by the aid of this theory, let us remember that the dogma and the Word of God are immutable, but that our knowledge is ephemeral.

The Bible, inspired by God to teach men the truths which shall lead us to our end, concerns itself neither with Ptolemy nor Copernicus; its object is not to teach us that the earth is round and the sun its centre. There is nothing to prove that when he wrote his sublime account of the creation, divided into six periods, and ending with the repose of the Eternal, Moses had any other intention than to put into the lips of his people a song which should perpetuate the remembrance of the greatest of all events, and put before the eyes of future generations a grand model of the typical week which was to rule the life of the Hebrew people.

Certain doctors, in a hurry to avenge the Bible from the attacks of a hostile Science, pretend that it speaks like Ptolemy; others like Galileo; this one like Cuvier; that like Elie de Beaumont, etc., etc. Such tactics can but bring into disrepute both Faith and the holy book. What would one think of a text that can be turned every way, and interpreted according to the most contradictory scientific systems? Nothing proves better to my mind that the Bible is not, strictly speaking, a scientific book; but an historical, moral, and religious one.

Leave the Word of God in His heaven; do not compromise it by abasing it upon earth; do not imprudently mingle it with the tempest of human thought. Misalliances are never worth anything: they do not raise those who pretend to raise themselves, and they abase those who are misallied.

The peasant remains a peasant, and the king's daughter is no more than the wife of him whom she marries.

You see at what price men of Science and believers can put an end to-day to the struggle which is tearing the very soul of the present generation.

Men of Science, the masters of youth, those who prepare them for public functions, themselves troubled and undecided, when they are not openly hostile, tell them nothing about God and Christ or the immortality of the soul; and, on the other hand, scandalized believers, horrified at the sight of the world's indifference and obliviousness of God, as it walks amongst paths intersected with precipices, amongst a refined and perfectly material civilization, utter cries of alarm and prophesy catastrophes.

We behold the growth of two hostile races: the sons of the earth, infatuated with materialized Science, rejecting God, and foolishly announcing that the time has come when the heavens are henceforth to be empty, and when the earth, transformed by man, will suffice for the reduced aspirations of disabused humanity; and the sons of Faith, who are animated by an indomitable hope, who, seeing the world transform itself by the action of terrestrial Science, believe with equal energy in the transformation of human Science by the action of the Gospel, and in the more overwhelming irradiation of the Word of God and of Christ, better interpreted and more profoundly known.

Which will vanquish?

Between these two races, that I may call—one horizontal and brutalized, the other vertical and moving to the Infinite—accord is not possible. The one will kill the other.

I say "kill" without alluding to violence or the sword; and to avoid equivocation I may say more properly, the one will *transform* the other. This is my Faith.

The struggle for existence, vital rivalry, is a sublime law; widely understood, it is undeniably the exact expression of that great fact, summed up by phenomena in the empire of life. Who triumphs in the struggle? who remains master in this rivalry? The bravest and the strongest. Translate, in speaking of intelligent beings, the most active, the most devoted, and the most enlightened.

This gives me hope for Thee, O Christ, and for the race descended from Thee. Has there arisen in the whole human family a being more enlightened than Thou? Has one arisen who can rival Thee in that absolute charity which Thou hast given for a law to thine own? And who has known better than Thou, to do and to suffer, even to the death, to prove whom Thou wert? From what ancestors are they descended who deny Thee? From whom are they raised up? When they are asked their master, where do they look? . . .

We fear neither the matter in which they glory, nor the anthropoid from which they believe themselves descended, nor the science with which they inflate themselves, nor the false liberty for which they cry out. Matter will be vanquished by the spirit of Him who has taught us to subdue the beast within us; and as that beast exists, it will be subdued, muzzled, and transformed.

The Science of earth will be re-allied to the Science of heaven: how shall that light which shines in the darkness of the human brain pretend to eclipse the splendour of which God Himself is the focus? That misunderstood liberty of those who, under its name, forge chains which the deceived multitude take for necklaces or bracelets, will be vanquished by that liberty, filled with the love of God, who loves men, and has inculcated a sublime fraternity. And how shall that liberty, which is governed by tyrannical passions and is coupled with hatred, pretend to vanquish that enfranchised liberty which is governed by love?

Open your heart to these hopes, O young man to whom your country seems to confide her future, and who works to raise and glorify her through peace. To hope is to live! And in these crises where all is at stake it is necessary to have a vitality above proof, and a surplus of hope. Be a man of hope and of great desires in order to be a man of great battles.

The prophet who, centuries before His advent, pointed to Christ, was praised by God Himself, who inspired him, as the man of desires, *vir desideriorum*. Thou whose soul, awakened and ardently engrossed with the work of Christ, waits His return amongst men; thou that workest to open Him a road amongst modern nations and new societies, seated in shadows of unbelief and in spiritual death, be like Daniel, the "man of desires," and steep in inviolable conviction the energy which makes thee brave, and the wisdom which leads to victory.

The work is urgent.

The day when we shall have discovered in Science the experimental truths which are its prize, and the false systems which corrupt it; the day when in matters of Faith we shall have put apart indisputable truths and human interpretations; the day when, well aware of the limits of the two domains, we shall neither mix up Science with Faith, nor Faith with Science, but, without confounding their means and their end, shall bring face to face these two orders of truth—on that day there will be light in every intellect. One can prophesy it: a new sun will shine in this sad age. Light will announce Peace, and Truth, which gives deliverance, will resuscitate Liberty with its indomitable vitality.

That day is near. There seems even now a speck of light upon the dark horizon.

Let us help this sunrise, if only by our wishes. Better than any one, we are convinced that wishes, before God, are worth more than our humble work.

Man prays and longs; God acts. What is the work of man? Almost nothing. What are his prayers and desires? Almost everything; for they move the sovereign action of the Infinite.

FIRST DISCOURSE.

POSITIVISM.

Brethren,
    It is not without emotion that I again come amongst you.

Time, which modifies, uses, and carries away everything in this world, has respected this labour of enlightenment at which we are working together: you in bringing to it that unbiased mind which is ready to sacrifice all to truth, and I in bringing before you the doctrine of God, that doctrine whose right understanding is the price of much watching, study, and prayer.

Those who have vowed themselves to this holy labour have an heroic task to accomplish. More than once their soul has been martyred and torn. You pity the labourer of the soil because he suffers; you esteem his activity and courage. Never pity the labourer of the truth; exalt him all the more, as his work is greater. One does not pity the martyr. Truth requires martyrs for her servants: she is conquered only by the very blood of the soul.

I attempted last year to give you an idea of the Catholic notion of man; to-day I speak to you of

God. Why of God? Ah, brethren, was there ever greater necessity for touching upon such a subject? If the idea of man is misunderstood, the idea of God is still more so.

Let us not deceive ourselves. It is not only the worship that is attacked, nor the temporal establishment of the Church that is threatened; it is not only the spirit of Christianity that they wish to remodel; it is something more: it is God Himself, it is the very corner-stone of all religion, that they want to shake and shatter. Perhaps you think that the idea of God should be left to philosophers to defend. No, brethren. We are the guardians of the temple; it belongs to us, rather than to the profane, to repair its ruins. Besides, where are the philosophers? Their voices are to-day dumb or impotent. Thus, the philosophers being no longer listened to, who shall defend God, if not the priest? He can defend Himself, you will say, and, besides, where are His enemies? They are everywhere. You can easily see it. To whom do the people of France go? To God? No. The lower classes turn away; they grovel upon the earth, while blaspheming heaven, and breaking the cross upon which Christ suffered death. By the side of this mass, carried away pell-mell, look at that brilliant and corrupt crowd, throwing itself into the arms of matter, to beg from it, not its subsistence, but unbridled enjoyment. That crowd is you, O civilized ones of this age, great forgetters of God, that the fever of business and of pleasure drags far away from Him and monopolizes.

Those men who think in this age, do they even raise their eyes to God? Look: the learned turn away from Him by thousands; absorbed in the study of phenomena, they forget the Principle; seduced by the attraction of secondary causes, they foolishly attempt to explain effects without the First Cause. Before, it was the despot who roused himself against God and His Christ. The parts are changed; to-day it is the learned who organize themselves together to intercept the Eternal Light, and close the paths which bring it to the human soul.

They have framed four grand systems in their war against God: scepticism, which by doubting reason doubts God; pantheism, which confounds nature and God; materialism, which places God in matter; positivism, which refuses to concern itself with the Infinite and the Absolute. Well, brethren, when the brute instinct blasphemes God, when civilization disdains Him, when atheistic Science banishes Him, have I not the right—what do I say?—is it not my duty to be His witness, to defend Him with all the poor science of which I am master, with all my reason and with all my faith?

This is my duty: to demolish first of all, one by one, all the systems of atheism; to establish scientifically the existence of the Divine Being; and to formulate concerning Him the true idea, such as is necessary to a mind capable of believing, of reasoning, and of experimenting—to a mind formed to adore, to love, and to pray to the Infinite.

I am confident, brethren, that you will support by

your intelligent sympathy, this work, which has no other ambition than the honour of our faith, and its defence against vain and dreary theories. Certain people see in Catholicism only a collection of rites, a pious routine ; they are tempted to despise it. Let us prove to them that it is the sublimest and most irrefutable of doctrines. The ignorant, corrupt souls, warped minds, despise the truth— so much the worse for them. We speak to loyal souls; and it is sufficient for the truth to be made apparent, to convince and re-ally those who are sincere.

It is expedient, brethren, to attack first of all that system, born only from yesterday, which in the name of Science dares to interdict the human mind from all search after God, and which, if it was true, would be the radical condemnation of all theodicy. I mean Positivism.

Be not surprised at the severity of my language in refuting it ; if it is necessary to justify it before you, I beg to remind you that it is one of those errors that a loyal reason can never brand with too great energy and indignation.

Considered doctrinally, Positivism is a system which professes to believe only those things which are accessible to experience. It will admit no other reality but matter, its properties and its forces, its phenomena and its laws. It only studies and aspires to know that which is to be seen, measured, and weighed. The rest it regards as hypothetical and outside the sphere of intelligence ;

from thenceforward it does not concern it. Observe, brethren, it does not deny, it does not affirm ; more reserved and more crafty, it does not concern itself in the matter, and if it is pressed to explain this strange attitude, it escapes by saying: " The invisible is not in my domain, nor within my cognizance."

Experience is its sole method. Reason to it is entirely experimental; it is only the faculty of entering into sensible relation with matter. To analyze, decompose, or compare facts ; to formulate under the name of laws, their consonance of similitude or of divergence, of succession or of simultaneity, by attempting syntheses always vaster and always insufficient—such is its work ; but it attempts in vain to penetrate the unique Law which all obeys. The unique Law is not where it searches for it. Its secret is to it closed.

This is the sum of this narrow doctrine, the most exclusive ever conceived by the brain of man. It is the most perfidious blow that has ever been struck, I do not say at faith, but at reason. From the moment that you profess only to admit matter, all that is not matter must be regarded as null and non-existent. Now, would you weigh the soul? or measure it? And God—who has weighed Him or measured Him? Who can describe His face or draw His outline? Therefore, as religion rests upon God and upon the soul, for a virile intelligence entering into Positivism there is neither God, nor soul, nor religion; they are old words, hollow legends from which a scientific mind is henceforth free. Humanity, according to Positivism, has for a long time amused itself with reveries without an object; they must be put an end to. " Science," says the master of the young school, " has put into retirement the Father of Nature, and it has just reconducted God to His own frontier, after thanking Him for His provisional services."

You see to what such a system would lead us. The defenders of Reason and Faith are warned. Let them rise up and keep guard; to-morrow, perhaps, it may be too late.

Positivism is as yet, even amongst the learned, but a small sect, but its spirit permeates everything—science, literature, the institutions and laws, private life and public life. The apparent certainty of its process, the fascination which matter and science exercise, the disgust of God which has possessed so many souls, the scepticism which enervates so many intellects—all contribute to put in fashion a theory which in other ages would not have aroused a glance of curiosity. If we do not seize it hand to hand, it will force itself upon us, it will govern us and go before us with authority. To-day daring, to-morrow it will be invincible. It must be conquered, examined in its relation to man, studied in itself, confronted with its own principles—judged, in fact, by the tenets it holds and from which it partly takes the secret of its strength.

In its relation to man, Positivism appears like a sacrilegious outrage. Studied in itself, it is in plain contradiction, and thus at the first shock breaks like iron when its granulation impedes the cohesion of the molecules. In its tenets Positivism is perfidious, it is disguised; it is weak because it dissembles. Let us, then, tear off the mask and not fear to expose and stigmatize this hypocritical doctrine.

Man has a right to judge all systems, measuring them by his own standard—as they give themselves out to be the perfection of his intelligence and the complement of his faculties, and that, summed up, they are made for him. Let Positivism appear, then, at the bar of the living conscience, and let it reply to her. Conscience will remain sovereign judge of those who wish to suppress God.

How does it treat man?

First of all, brethren, it ignores his religious aspirations; it tortures and insults that which is the most sublime and sacred part of man. This is its first crime. One cannot long mistake those legitimate instincts, those complex energies which move and engross our very being. No matter what may be the blindness of passion or the illusion of false systems, the slightest glance, in an hour of clear vision and sincerity, is sufficient to show us the grand dimensions of our nature, and to shadow forth all that it contains of the immortal and infinite.

Well, I ask you, what is the predominant longing in you? what is at once the highest and most indestructible aspiration?

Is it the wish to vegetate, to have your daily bread, in order not to faint on the way? You deceive yourselves, brethren; "man does not live by bread alone."

What is the satiety of the body to me if the soul is empty? And what matters its hunger if the soul is satisfied?

But what can satisfy the soul? Nothing created; neither riches nor pleasure, neither glory nor power, neither Science nor, even, virtue. There is in it a still higher longing, a divine hunger that the Infinite alone can appease. Whosoever has not felt this sublime hunger has not been born into the grand life of man; and whosoever by any possibility has succeeded in stifling it ought, at the same time, to have ceased to live. The observer who takes no account, in the intimate life of man or the general life of humanity, of this great phenomenon, has seen only the surface of our nature.

Now, brethren, what place does Positivism give in its doctrine to the want, to what I may fearlessly call the passion, for God? Does it explain it? Does it even speak of it? Yes, it speaks of it, but to destroy it; yes, it endeavours to explain, but only to condemn and thrust it away. This leaning towards the Infinite is without an object— according to it; this hunger an illusion; this sacred aspiration an infirmity, almost a madness. "What dost thou seek above the earth," it says to us in contemptuous accents, "thou foolish creature, so slow to quit the illusions of childhood? What is the use of gazing fixedly upon that illimitable horizon? It is impenetrable. Be wise, therefore, and learn to circumscribe thyself. Thou canst not attain to that immensity which fascinates and tortures thee; put a veil across thine eyes, and, instead of allowing thy vain contemplation to stray into the heavens, look at the earth and conquer it. Heaven was not made for thee; the earth is thy only domain." By what right, in truth, are such decrees formulated? Why repudiate noble and invincible tendencies? Your doctrine cannot explain them—does that mean that it must deny them? Facts are not to be bent to your systems; your systems must be in accordance with fact.

Supposing it was sufficient, in order to appease the vehemence of its longings, to say to the soul, "Be calm;" but who could possibly compress their nature thus? It is ever pushing forwards: who can at their pleasure drag it back? It rises to God: who can prevent it from reaching towards the Infinite? Even if one could, has one the right? But one neither has the power nor the right. It is well for Positivism to know that it, no more than Epicurus of old, can succeed in putting a stop to our heavenward aspirations, and binding us down to what can be seen, weighed, and measured. It may say "nothing *is* but matter"—we do not believe it. In spite of ourselves the Infinite torments us. Matter? it overwhelms us. Matter? in the end it disgusts us. All these systems, with their sacrilegious pretensions of limiting us to themselves, are too narrow for the greatness of our soul. If logic did not vanquish them, the expansion of our divine vitality would be sufficient to shatter them; human nature is an ocean without limit, and they would not even be as the rock which restrains the wave and provokes its fury in the attempt to arrest it.

Let us now see, my brethren, to what mutilation of reason—the master faculty of man—Positivism lends itself; this is its second crime.

As a religious being, man reclaims the Infinite; as a reasonable being, he wants Truth; he seeks for it in every direction, and only seeks to know it in order to live in its light. Now, reason in the pursuit of truth executes three principal acts. By the first she experiments, and by casting herself upon things outside, she seizes phenomena, analyzes them, compares them, and discovers their laws. By the second she turns within herself, attentive to the facts of her perception; she argues, discourses, rises to the very substance and cause, and contemplates by the rays of a higher light those eternal and necessary truths without which it would be impossible even to think. Lastly, by the third she enters into religious connection with the Cause of causes, the Absolute Principle of being, which deigns to reveal Itself to her; and, without being able to measure or comprehend It, she perceives It, affirms It, listens to It, adores It. All Science is in the first act, all philosophy in the second, all the faith of believers in the third. They are joined in an indissoluble harmony; they are superposed and appeal to each other; to isolate is to weaken them. How can I experiment without being furnished with those immutable principles which are the condition of all experience? How can I conceive these supreme axioms to which my thoughts are obedient, without going back to the focus from whence these narrow, divided, and broken rays have escaped to shine within and around me.

These truths ought, by their very clearness, to force themselves upon the mind. But that is nothing! Sophism has every audacity; at will it sows shadows before it, and covers its steps with night, in order to conceal the attack more surely, and to surprise what it dares not confront. Do you know the tactics of the Positivists? In their arbitrary dogmatism they have proclaimed this: "Those questions which concern the origin and end of things are outside the pale of human comprehension, and consequently can no longer direct the inquiries of the mind, the conduct of man, or the development of society. As to the origin of things, we were not there; to the end of things we have not yet arrived. We have, therefore, no means of knowing either this origin or this end."

Tired of ancient systems that an impotent philosophy built and rebuilt incessantly, disabused of the religious conceptions of humanity which they treat as childish dreams, they teach that experience is the only light, and have decreed the admission of that alone as true which it controls: and all is said.

But, my brethren, this is just the point: Positivism affirms, it must also *prove*. Experience is only a third of complete reason. That to which it cannot attain, speculative reason may discover. Where the feet of man cannot tread, its wings may bear it.

In a living nature it is not allowable to suppress a part. Although a faculty may unsettle us by its digressions, or disconcert us by its weakness, it must yet be respected. It must be restrained or stimulated, not suppressed. What is true of a faculty is not less so of its functions. To paralyze one is an offence against nature. And it is you, you men of Science, defenders of the light, who would raise this homicidal hand against human reason; it is you who would only preserve its least function, that lower function which puts it in contact with matter; it is you who would forbid its most vigorous impulse—that by which it enters into itself, and the sublime impetus which unites it to the absolute Principle.

You will not succeed. You are only deniers, deniers to the utmost; and humanity, while contemning you, will always reply in the words of Shakespeare: "There are more things in heaven and earth, Horatio, than are dreamt of in your philosophy!"

After all, what is a doctrine of which the basis is so weak, and which in order to seduce can invoke neither sternness of logic nor grandeur of conception?

When materialism, with Condillac, sought to

deduce everything from a transformed Primordial sensation, there was in this work a power of analysis which might attract more than one mind. When pantheism wished to establish the consubstantial unity of the finite with the Infinite, pantheism was enabled to seduce more than one religious soul that found in that the ideal of its dreams, and more than one exacting reason which the dualism of creation had staggered. When, in the presence of redoubtable contradictions which arose between the experimental world and rational conception, reason began to doubt itself, and did not recoil even from suicide, there was, even in this work of death, a funereal grandeur—the grandeur of Samson crushed beneath the ruins of the temple whose columns he had himself destroyed. But in Positivism there is nothing grand, nothing fine, nothing alluring. I see in it only the work of withered and discouraged minds, *blasé* souls in which long commerce with matter has blunted all sense of the divine.

And that is why, brethren, we reject and condemn it, in the name of Faith, and also in the name of Reason, in the name of God and also of man. It is man more than God that is endangered by this narrow doctrine, whose whole genius consists in dissimulating, beneath a materialized learning, a system of dreadful negation.

Let us quit, now, these lofty regions of speculative reason : because of its sublimity it is, perhaps, not accessible to all minds. Let us enter into practical and moral life; for Positivism, not content with reducing all the natural sciences to experience, pretends to bring into the same limits moral Science itself, in order to render it as certain and solid as physical Science. Here no one can be indifferent; we are in the presence of that which is man's peculiar glory and entitles him most to respect, which alone can elevate him above all else —I mean virtue and morality.

What does Positivism do with morality, virtue, and conscience?

The object of morality is the inclination of every free and intelligent man towards good. What is good? This is for practical reason to teach, and conscience to command. When this light shines forth, liberty finds its master. To obey this master is our first duty; to *be able* to follow it our most sacred right, and the unattackable basis of our independence. Nothing can fetter us and say, "Thou shalt not do good." Conscience is supreme; she gives commands, but receives none, save from God. Neither despotism, nor passion, nor sophism can long succeed in stifling this voice, which is the echo of God's. Despotism will tire itself out, passion be silent, and sophistry dulled; and man, sooner or later, will understand that for him repose and honour are only to be found in the acceptation of the imperative mandates of conscience.

Above every other idea, there arises within us, brethren, the grand one of duty, of moral obligation. It does not confound itself with the useful;

it has nothing in common with the necessary. And, indeed, brethren, what is the useful? That which must be done under pain of suffering. What is the necessary? That which must be done under pain of death. And the obligatory? Listen; some one says to you, "Act against your conscience, or you die." Would you submit yourself to this immoral and iniquitous order? Would you violate your conscience? No. Invincible in your right, you would say to the executioner, "Strike if you will: I know how to suffer, I know how to die; but I will not betray my duty." This, brethren, is the obligatory. And, if it is necessary to define it in words, I should say, The obligatory is that which must be done even at the cost of suffering or of death.

Well, I defy Positivism to explain the law of morality and its character of absolute obligation. Imprisoned by prejudice in experience, it is to experience alone that it can have the right to appeal. Let it observe and compare facts, let it analyze them at will, let it multiply and torture them; facts will not furnish it with the absolute divine notion of duty and right. Experience may reveal to us in matter the useful and the necessary, but never the obligatory. It is given us only by conscience and practical reason. The one reveals to us what is good: it may hold a different language according to the age, the degree of culture, the race, and the genius of those it teaches. The other binds us to good; laws change, nations disappear, ages pass away, but that obligation remains immutable; and the chains forged by conscience are everywhere and always of the same divine metal.

The best fortified scepticism is constrained to capitulate before the law of duty, and to recognize its absolute character; if not, moral order is shaken to its very foundation, and not one stone is left upon another. Kant well understood this—he, the audacious sceptic, who shook human reason with an arm of iron, and drove out the most sublime and necessary truths in the name of his implacable logic. After having accumulated so many ruins, he paused before duty and confessed its objective reality, and, convinced that all should bow before the good, he said, not without grandeur and enthusiasm, "Two things fill the soul with an ever-renewed admiration and respect, which increases as thought reverts to them oftener and applies itself to them more closely: the starry heavens above us, and the moral law within."

If Positivism wishes to remain faithful to its principles—and it pretends to do so—if it wishes to be logical, and not, like Kant, destroy with one hand and build up again with the other, there is an end for it of all duty and virtue; it is perforce confined to that egotism of which interest is the rule, and to that fatalism of which brute force is the law.

Let it not attempt to shirk these consequences. It speaks, I know, of instincts, of wants, even of sentiments; it takes account of the *altruistic* tendency, as it calls it in its barbaric language: but, brethren, is that duty? Duty is neither an instinct, a want, a sentiment, nor a tendency; it is an absolute rule, the expression of the necessary connection between an intelligent being and its supreme law. It is either so or not. If Positivism wishes to use the exact sense of the word, let it first tell us of the supreme end of liberty. Its principles will defend it. Experience and observation, to which it pretends to reduce everything, cannot go beyond the limited circle of matter; and whoso wishes to come at the final aim of man and his liberty of action, must have the wise audacity to overstep by reason the domain of experience—it must recognize the soul and confess a God.

Before this boldness Positivism recoils. But, my brethren, when duty and moral obligation are suppressed in the human conscience, what remains? When, instead of seeing in it a reflex of the divine law, its character of absolute truth is taken away to reduce it to the level of useful convention, or a habit gradually contracted by our forefathers and become the inalienable inheritance of a race, again I say, what becomes of humanity? Give to a man thus despoiled the iron muscle of a beast of prey; give him a strength of will which neither fear, suffering, nor death can abate; give him an intelligence which could scrutinize the most impenetrable secrets of nature, and the genius to divine them—you would not have filled up the void; you would not have given the man that which is his sole honour and chiefest glory. What matters the vigour of muscle, or energy of character, or sublimity of genius? That which is required before everything else in human nature—and no one here will contradict me in this—is the sentiment of moral law, the conscience which dictates it, and the virtue which remains faithful to it even to death itself.

This, brethren, is the secret of heroes and saints, those firm yet gentle hearts, the salvation of nations in their extremity, the strength of a worn-out race, the glory of the humanity which beholds, and the God who created them.

When a doctrine, be it even the most intelligent of doctrines, does not fear to touch this holy ark, it is superfluous to argue; it is sufficient to confound it, to draw down upon it the glance of the just, that glance whose serenity condemns without appeal, and brands all that would outrage conscience and virtue.

Be yourselves those just ones, you who have in the depths of your souls the sentiment of duty, and that inexorable conscience which binds you to it even to martyrdom!

At the sight of these ruins accumulated with such violence, you perhaps ask yourselves, and I ask it also with you: Is Positivism a firmly united system, and one whose basis is solid? Has it in its favour the logic of deduction? If so, it must be in the right, and we shall be forced to acknowledge its power.

Neither the one nor the other. Positivism is in flagrant contradiction with its own principles.

This system, in effect, admits the experimental alone as an object, and recognizes no other faculty but experience and observation. All that is outside observed facts, all that is not contained in time and space, that double sphere which embraces all experience, is for it abstract and without reality. Has it not said so? " The absolute is a chimera; if it exists it is beyond our reach." And the decisive reason it invokes for proscribing metaphysic and theodicy is that both have the absolute as their object.

If, then, it is proved that on its own showing, by experimenting and observing that matter to which it would limit us, it leaves the relative and touches upon the absolute; if it is demonstrated that it works by means of the absolute, will it not be placed in full contradiction with itself? That is just the point I wish to bring forward. What is the absolute? There are no two ways of taking it: it is that which *is* of itself, immutable, necessary, without condition of time and place, that which has been, which is, and which will be. Now, the nature of human intelligence is such, that it cannot judge of and comprehend the contingent and variable but by the aid of the necessary, the immutable, the eternal. It is impossible to experiment upon matter without by experience you employ absolute principles. You must employ mathematics, as you want to count, to measure, to weigh, and to calculate. Now, the principles of mathematics, of algebra, of geometry, and of dynamics, are something absolute and unconditional; they are above time and space, outside all experience, and it is needless to have proved them in all time and all space to be certain of their immutable truths. You require logic; then the logical principles of identity and contradiction which govern our intelligence in the smallest experimental labour are immutable and absolute: they belong to the very essence of thought. You require ontological, that is, metaphysical principles. We believe in an order, a law which regulates all the phenomena of nature; and, without having proved it even, we know that neither this order will fail nor this law belie itself. It is absolute. We believe in the principle of causality, we know that given such and such a cause, such and such an effect must follow; and if by any chance, the conditions remaining identical, the result is not the same, we judge our experience defective, and rectify by the absolute principle of causality that experience to which Positivism would lead and subordinate everything.

Therefore there is something else besides experiment and phenomena. All experiments, as you have seen, presuppose absolute principles which throw a light upon, and at need correct them. Therefore when Positivism affirms that experiment is everything, and makes use on its own showing of absolute principles which govern it, Positivism contradicts itself. One may excuse everything in a system; one may in the name of logic even forgive absurdity; but a system in contradiction with its own principles stands self-accused.

Positivism well recognizes this extremity to which a severe examination can reduce it. All those mathematical, logical, and ontological axioms which are the very essence of reason have been put before it: that absolute which incommodes it, and from which it cannot free itself, has been cast in its teeth. "It is merely provisionary," is the reply. "We construct an edifice, and the principles of which you speak are merely the scaffolding, observed and classified facts are the monument. The work once accomplished, the scaffolding falls and the monument alone remains." Positivism deceives itself, it confounds the scaffolding with the genius of the architect, and the mould of the statue with the ideal of the sculptor. What is this which is provisionary but lasts for ever? These principles and axioms, are they not my very reason itself? To suppress them would it not be to annihilate it? One must be singularly determined to regard everything from the lowest point of view not to comprehend that the first principles of reason are but a reflex of the living substantial and personal absolute which alone can explain them. This absolute is the terror of Positivism; it would rather contradict itself than recognize a God; we, vanquished by the truth, would rather recognize God than contradict ourselves.

This attitude will foreshadow to you, brethren, the doctrinal tenets of Positivism; it is on this last point that it will now be necessary to examine it.

Every system is a living organism. It has a

peculiarity which in characterizing it reveals its genius. If you allow yourself to be persuaded by is title you will only see in Positivism a system very positive in its aim and very positive in its method. The title is deceptive. I always distrust those names given to doctrines; they too often hide what they ought to reveal.

Go beyond appearances, sift well this theory which gives itself out to be the highest achievement of our intellectual maturity, and what will you find? First of all, materialism. Materialism consists in recognizing nothing as real but matter, consequently it denies the soul's existence. Now, Positivism, by virtue of its own principles, cannot overstep the circle of matter and raise itself to the consideration of a soul. "I do not assert the soul's existence," it will tell you, "and I do not deny it: I abstain from the word and am indifferent to the thing." What matters this plea of non-admission? Whoever affirms that there is no other means of perceiving but by experience must hold as non-existent all that goes beyond it. It is proved, then, that for Positivists limited to experimental Science the soul is an empty word. Indeed, do they not say so in their books? Open their dictionaries and read: "The soul is only the conjunction of the functions of the brain and the marrow." Do you hear this, brethren. Taking that matter which is called the nervous substance, observing that to this matter are attached certain phenomena of vitality and sensibility, the Positivists concede that there is a soul, in the sense that the brain and the spinal marrow exercise certain functions which have been placed under the heading of the word soul. And they think after that to escape from the reproach of materialism! For my part I see but one difference between the two doctrines: on the one side frankness, on the other dissimulation. It is better to have error without cloak, than these hypocritical sophisms that seem ashamed of themselves, and wear a mask to deceive the better. This is not all: it is atheistic. Directly experience is put forward as the exclusive principle, one is in atheism. God cannot be experimented on or tested, any more than the soul can. The soul transcends that matter which serves as its organ. God transcends all phenomena whose multitude and variety compose the universe. And in the same way that Positivism is compelled to deny the soul—as its method cannot touch it—so is it forced to suppress God. "But no!" it cries. "I don't deny God. I don't affirm Him. I don't concern myself about Him." Do you see how it escapes? The materialist denies, the sceptic doubts, the Positivist evades. The first says, "God is not," or "God is but matter." The second, "I don't know." It says, "I neither deny nor affirm." "What do you do then?" "I abstain." "Very well: but know that to abstain is the hypocrite's way of denying." You are worse than materialists, worse if possible than atheists: you are the very destroyers of reason. On the pretext of strengthening it on its base you have brought it down to the level of matter. You have taught it to doubt that movement by which it falls back upon itself and the impetus which transports it heavenward to seek for its origin. And it is you that have begun this dark age in which enfeebled intelligence turns to experimentalism, and will behold nothing but facts and the laws of facts.

Materialism, atheism, scepticism, that is what, logically, Positivism implies. But, brethren, it will not even say so frankly. No, it must keep to the very end its dissimulation. Let us tear off the mask, and treat it for what it is. What is this prudishness in error? Whoso refuses to see in thought anything else but a property of the nervous tissue denies the soul; whoso will not confess God, denies Him; whoso will not make use of total reason, denies reason: it is whole, or it does not exist. If Positivism is true, God and the soul must be declared unknowable, inaccessible; if it is false, let us declare it as such and let not inattentive souls believe it. Let us charge straight at the enemy, and no longer allow it in the name of Science to make a void in heaven by banishing God—exorcising Him as it blasphemously declares. God gone, truth also goes, genius is eclipsed, right is withered, justice dies, and virtue follows these divine exiles. What remains? Man. But man reduced to animality, a sort of learned dog, who knows how to read, to classify, and to perpetuate itself; to whom one asks whence he comes, and who answers you, "I don't know;"—whither he goes, and who answers, "What does it matter?"—who he is—and who, to resolve the problem, seeks, bent towards the earth to which he has debased himself, ties of relationship with the animals, instead of raising his head to discover in the Infinite titles of divine affiliation.

Brethren, we have condemned Positivism, it remains for us to confound it.

Would you believe it, this strange doctrine which is, being defined, the negation of God and the soul, pretends to have its religion, and wishes to adore something: so difficult is it to restrain that longing to worship which is the very essence of our nature. And do you know what certain Positivists, the most fervent and mystic of the sect, have worshipped? Do you know what they offer to the worship of adepts? God? the human soul? they have denied both. What then can they put on an altar? Only matter remains, and that humanity which proceeds from it. They take this matter and this humanity and say, Here is our God! What! this materialized humanity, going about in darkness on the surface of a planet, covered in rags, made up of misery and vice, of egotism and ferocity; or this other joyful humanity, not less miserable, all engrossed by its feasts and pleasures: it is *that* that we must salute as God? Never! Even if humanity had all Science as guide, I would not worship it: for human Science is fallible. If it had all strength for its sceptre, I would not worship it; for strength is tyrannical. If humanity had every virtue as its nimbus, I would not worship it! one can worship nothing created.

What humanity can you present for the adoration of man? Ah, I have just told you—humanity without God. It has money, it is true; and power and pleasure, Science even, and indefinite progress, but without God it will never be but dust and filth.

Yes, man without God, this is the god enthroned in this unhappy land. If she succumbs in despair it is because she is enslaved before this shameful altar—if she is agitated by nameless convulsions it is because she is seized with the chill of death under the shadow of that idol! Let me break it!

Positivism will disavow it, perhaps, and say this is not what she dreamed. That is possible, but it is none the less her work. And besides, is there so great a distance between her ideal humanity with which it began, and that vile humanity with which it ends?

As we must adore something, let us not adore what is inferior nor what is degraded. Let us adore nothing human, nothing created. Adore the Eternal God who through love took upon Himself in Jesus Christ a flesh without spot and was crucified for us. He broke all bonds; He freed our people and our race; He raised up the most noble sentiments and the most heroic virtues; He made this land: while the god which they would give us disorganizes, dishonours, and kills it.

Continue in this sacrilegious worship, and prepare to die. We are already very low. At the foot of this vile and funereal altar we already devour each other. This grim feast will soon be consummated. O God, permit it not! Let this doctrine of nothingness pass away like some unhealthy vapour. Let Thy truth, O God, reappear amongst us to save this people that is dying, because it loves Thee not: and that loves Thee not, because it knows Thee not.

SECOND DISCOURSE.

MATERIALISM.

BRETHREN,

Positivism ventures to say to man, hungering for God, "Thy reason is only capable of exploring matter. To go away from experience is to leave reason behind. If God exists, what does it matter to thee? Those paths which lead to God are closed to thee." But, my brethren, one cannot thus suppress the growth of a living being, and in the name of man's most sacred aspiration, in the name of morality, in the name even of Science, we have rejected this impotent doctrine. It would seem that the road should now be open to us, and that we can, unfettered, search after the Infinite. Not so. A system, the brother of Positivism, arrests us. This one does not destroy the path, he opens it wide; he does not ascend, he descends; he does not seek for the cause from above, he persistently places it beneath; he confounds the starting point with the principle, that which begins with that which produces, matter with thought, the atom with God. He does not say, "In the beginning was the Word, and the

Word was God;" he says, "In the beginning was the atom, and the atom is God." *

Question this system a little.

"What exists?" Matter. Is there anything outside matter? Nothing. Is there no God? No. Then all that is, is matter? You have said it: matter is the real God. It is eternal, indestructible in its forces, in perpetual movement, and undergoing wondrous changes in its mobile form. And man, whence comes he? From matter. Whither does he go? To matter. Has he a soul? No. Is he immortal? No. Then he ends? After some few years. But intelligence? A secretion of the brain. Liberty? An illusion; everything is predestined. Virtue? A calculation, a mere suggestion of interest. Devotion? I don't know what you mean: an affair of interest, a fortunate passion.

You shudder, brethren. Well, this is Materialism —this is it without exaggeration. Materialists themselves, if there are any here, will have the loyalty to recognize it. Behold it in its naked brutality, despoiled of the artifice of language, of all scientific apparel, isolated from those facts whose novelty and able assistance dupe and dazzle unreflective minds. What more is needed to condemn it in the name of simple common sense? Nevertheless, I will do it the honour of a less summary discussion and a more profound refutation.

* "The atom," says M. Büchner, "or the most minute indivisible and fundamental part of matter, is the God to whom the highest and lowest existence owes its being.—" Force and Matter."

Every doctrine implies three elements: principle, deduction, and practical consequence. The principle must be clear; the deductions logical; the consequence moral. Now, brethren, Materialism is without clearness in its principles, illogical in its deductions, and immoral in its consequences; I will prove it. It is necessary that its cause should be well heard and conscientiously judged. It is rampant in this country. Many men have mutilated their reason, thinking to enfranchise it; but many more have turned to matter, and, fascinated by it, have buried there their soul and their God. There is only a school of positivists, there is a whole nation of Materialists.

They are scarcely worthy of pity, these little minds whose soul is too great a burden for them; these unnatural sons who, in a henceforth empty heaven, desire neither a Father nor a God. Their errors engender corruption and stir up revolt. You are indignant, brethren; I, a priest, pity them. You would punish, I would rather heal them; and, in the very depths of my soul, I find for those who bear the torch and lead the work of corruption, more commiseration than anger or contempt.

And, first of all, behold the principles of Materialism, the apparently unshakable basis of a system which requires from our treacherous senses a truth which reason alone can reveal to us. "There is only matter and force. No matter without force, and no force without matter. Matter and force are inseparable. Nothing is destroyed, nothing is created; that which is has always been, that which has been will always be. Force and matter are eternal."

What more vague and arbitrary, more hypothetical and ill-founded? You shall convince yourselves of this. This matter, which Materialism thinks it knows so well, and to which it has recourse to explain everything, is itself enwrapped in an impenetrable veil of mystery, and is all the more surely concealed as it appears to be the more easy to discover. What is matter? I ask the most expert Materialist, the most competent modern Science; certes, it has every right to answer me, this Science which explores matter with such ability, and with a zeal and constancy which the defenders of Faith may justly envy.

Matter is that which is felt, is seen, is palpable, is weighed, and is measured. Here is a mineral; you look at it, you find it a certain colour. Very good. You weigh it, you find it a certain weight. Very good. You analyze it in your crucible, you make the elements of which it is composed declare themselves: a simple body called carbon, a simple body called oxygen. Very good. You take some water; you analyze it, you declare it to be composed of hydrogen and oxygen in strictly determined proportions, and you think you have the secret when you say, Water is burnt and oxydized hydrogen. Very good. You say of this, it is an element; of that, it is an acid; of this crystalline substance, it is a salt. Good. But, my brethren, up to this what have you done? You have simply verified subjective phenomena produced upon you by an exterior cause, of whose nature you are still absolutely ignorant. You have, first of all, considered a colour. Colour is not external to you; it is *in* you: yellow, red, and blue are simple modifications of our sensibility; their cause alone is objective. And even, to speak exactly, the objects have precisely every colour but that which our senses lend them. It is thus with taste, with heat, and with cold. Isolate the objects from the sensation they produce, and by what do they make known their action and presence, what remains to them? Their weight. But what is weight? A resistance, a movement in antagonism with yourself. What is a movement? Primarily this supposes a force, experience has not yet verified it; and what becomes of matter if you identify it with force?

Thus you see yourself obliged to take from matter one by one those attributes with which you benevolently invested it, and by means of which you flattered yourself you would know it. But when you have thus despoiled it of those qualities which are in yourself, of cold and heat, sound, light, weight, movement, purely subjective sensations, again, what remains? The "I don't know" of Fénélon, "which crumbles in the hand as you press it." Thus, what these superficial minds imagine to be the clearest, is in reality the most dense.

There remains at least extension, you will say. Let us see if extension is not itself a formation of our mind, a relative manner of considering things. Kant has affirmed it: is it easy to refute this successfully ? Extension of matter presupposes atoms; if atoms are not simple, of what are they themselves composed ? If they are simple, how do they explain extension ? Well, I concede you the objective reality of extension, I also concede movement and impenetrability. You think, perhaps, that you have now grasped intangible matter ? Take care, these attributes will confound each other ; extension supposes the impenetrability of the atom, and impenetrability supposes movement; for it cannot be conceived without resistance, and resistance implies movement. Thus nothing remains but a thing capable of movement, otherwise a force. What force ?

Is this clear ? You have listened to me, brethren, with an attention which astonishes me, and for which I thank you. What have you beheld ? The transformation of matter into force. Having made an abstraction of the subject considered, we have just convinced ourselves that there is in matter neither heat, cold, light, obscurity, sound, nor silence. There remains, Science itself proclaims, but motion, and a grand mechanism which wisely determines its laws and conditions.

But if matter is identical with force, what becomes of Materialism, which pretends to oppose the one to the other ? What becomes of its famous principle of their inseparable union ? A pure tautology ! Are systems, then, founded upon tautologies?

I have insisted upon these preliminaries because

Materialism is most careful in defining its principles. Turn to those books which teach it; they will solemnly assure you that force and matter are united. You ask in vain what are matter and force—they will not deign to answer you. They prove by this calculated silence that the starting-point of their theory is obscure, and that they wish to make use of this obscurity to the benefit of the cause. That is why, when one wishes to vanquish a doctrine, one must at all cost exact a clear definition of its principles.

What is that force which, according to the Materialists, is always united with matter? There are four forces in the world. Mechanical force, which you prove every day and every hour; it comes into play with the least muscular action. Physico-chemical force, evidenced in the combination and decomposition of bodies. Vital force, shown in every organized living being. Spiritual force, that of thought and free will, of which we all are conscious.

Of which force do the Materialists speak? Of spiritual? It is false. There are beings who do not think, who have no free will. Of vital force? It is false. Certain things have no life. Of mechanical? It is contestable. Of what force then? The only one which cannot be contested is physico-chemical force. I concede, then, to Materialism this limited and defined starting point. I accord it an extended matter and a physico-chemical force. If that is its meaning I have cleared up what it sets forth as a fundamental dogma.

But before going further let us see what there is arbitrary and hypothetical in this dogma.

What has told the Materialists that this force and this matter are eternal? Experience? It is not in a position to fathom Eternity, even to speak of it. Chained to time and space it cannot depart from them. We have been present, it is true, at no creation, or total destruction, but what matter? Is it a condition of the truth of things that man must have witnessed their birth in his crucibles, or put them in the field of his telescopes? It is by these vague gratuitous hypotheses that Materialism has sought to find an answer to every thing. Let us see it at work: you will soon see what a breach it makes in reason, and what becomes in its hands of the principle of causality, that all-powerful lever with which human intelligence raises the world of the unknown.

It is a prodigious work that which a system undertakes whose professed doctrine is to explain the universality of beings. Positivism is more prudent; it takes care to explain nothing. The Materialist is more daring; he disdains the perfidious timidity of the positivist. "I admit only matter," says he, "and its mechanical and physico-chemical forces. With that I explain every thing—the origin, the end, and the law of the universe. No mysteries for me. I know how things begin, how they develop, where they end." You will say this pretension seems exorbitant. Well, open a

Materialistic book, you will see that it is a formal one. Does the result answer to these ambitious pretensions? I will make you the judges, brethren.

If matter was motionless, the task of the Materialist would be easy. He would only have to say, " Matter is : it persists in the immutability of its forces, and the uniformity of a time which measures, without adding to it." Man proves it. Why should he seek for more? Certainly where there is no progressive evolution there is nothing new ; where there is nothing new, there is nothing to stimulate the intelligence of man and provoke his curiosity. But matter moves ; it develops ; and Science, in clearing up the past in which ages count but as minutes, where used-up worlds have cast their *débris*, penetrates also the future, it sees that which will be as that which has been ; and its prophetic glance envelops matter in the indefatigable unfolding of its growing creations. It is first of all a formless chaos. Whether you observe it in the immensity of the heavens where it escapes our action, or whether you analyze it in the delicate crucibles, in which you can crush it for an instant, to oblige it to follow its inevitable laws, and tell you the names of its hidden forces, matter diffuse and shadowy soon submits to the mechanical, physical, or chemical force inherent to its nature.

See over your head this immense nebula, this *magma* splendid with fire and light. Suddenly a point of concentration is formed in this mass ; it is the embryon of a solar system. Here is a centre. This cosmic mass reorganizes and rearranges itself.

Other points of concentration arise in its midst which operate with the same energy. By virtue of gravitation and universal attraction these divers centres separate according to their density and their mass, and they describe around each other those gigantic orbits whose laws constitute the dynamics of heaven.

Look closer to you, in your crucible. This is no longer the infinitely great, but the infinitely small : no longer suns, but molecules and imponderable atoms. Imperceptible elements are joined in definite and multiple proportion, and in invariable quantities. Always the same quantity of oxygen combined with the same quantity of hydrogen or carbon. To these inevitable laws matter, whatever its dimensions, is never disobedient. Under their empire explosive gases are restrained; liquids of unstable equilibrium round their surface; and solids commence, by deposit, that marvel which is called the world of crystals. Always and everywhere molecules group themselves in regular and mysterious forms, as though a multitude of geometers pulled them by a cord, in order that in all their fairy combinations the atoms should not stray from the ideal line they have to follow.

Suns roll in space in splendid constellation; atoms tremble in the rigid frame in which mechanism has imprisoned them. All at once, in the midst of these celestial worlds and surprised atoms, a living being palpitates—a substance without fixed form, floating undecided, drawing to it the elements which it modifies and rejects after transforming them. Behold the protoplasma, life in its rudimentary form. Soon living matter, composed of hydrogen, oxygen, carbon, and azote, is condensed; it takes a centre and an envelope, it becomes cellular. The cellule is the living being *par excellence*. It is with it that the spirit of life works, and in it it rests. Joined to other cellules, it composes with them all life, its tissues, organs, and covering. A wondrous architect, this simple element suffices to build innumerable edifices, *chef-d'œuvres* of co-ordination and solidity, which it animates in a moment.

Matter lives at first but as a grain. It forms the lovely fleece of the bare earth, its garment of verdure woven by the hand of an invisible artist. But do you know what has happened? Blind forces arise here and there; the central fire of the planet ill-contained bursts forth; mechanism enters roughly into play; the primitive flora is carbonized and swallowed up; life has capitulated to that which has no life, and that which was a centre has become a tomb. After this first triumph of force, life is renewed more brilliantly; the earth is covered with a rarer vegetation. In this less burning dust under these more firmly rooted trees animal life appears. Under the incessant and progressive work of life the nervous substance becomes elaborated. It forms itself into a singular appearance which is called the brain. Thanks to this powerful organ, life is not simply the faculty of nourishing itself, of consuming, and elaborating within itself what it takes in the exterior world; it is the faculty of imprinting in itself the immaterial image of things, of feeling, and of knowledge. This higher and mysterious life is, nevertheless, not the last act of matter. One day upon the earth, Science can tell you, in the midst of the primitive fauna and flora, the one mute, the other noisy, both unconscious, an unheard-of phenomenon arrives. Intelligence appears. There arrives, in all the nobility and royal pride of stature, a splendid being who names things, who knows them, who speaks as a master and can lead them. One sees the being who thinks, wills, and is free—man!

The animal has sensation; man has thought. The animal can neither reason nor reflect; it sees effects without comprehending the cause. Man goes back to the principle, and looks forward to the consequence. The animal has but appetites, wants, and passions. Man possesses aspirations, will, and love. The animal is egotistic; man may be disinterested. The one is inevitably impelled, the other is master of himself; and, as he belongs to himself, he can give himself through devotion and sacrifice, even to death. Although, like the animal, he touches matter, he is not absorbed by it; and in him there is the divine. His thought is a reflex of the Eternal Intelligence; his will an impulse of the Infinite Mind; and his soul the image and resemblance of God. Upon these heights, at this *chef-d'œuvre*, are arrested the progressive evolution of things, and the marvellous Odyssey of matter.

Well, brethren, it is here that I look for Materialism. Matter is in chaos; it organizes itself. The infinitely great become constellated, the infinitely small crystallized; life germinates, sensation quivers; thought shines like a new star; will is in free movement towards the Infinite: all is in motion —Science proves it. Let Materialism then explain this progressive movement. Let us not forget that it admits only mechanical, physical, or chemical forces. I summon it to render account of the formation of the heavens and the earth, of animal and vegetable life; I summon it to render account of thought, of liberty, and of love.

What a task, my brothers! Is it possible? The universe in its development, see you not, moves from the less to the greater, from the imperfect to the perfect? Matter harmonized in its crystalline form is a progression from chaotic matter; life is in progression from the reign of brute force; sensibility is in progression from life; thought and love are in progression from sensibility. Now, it is from the starting-point, from the atom, that the Materialist pretends to take all this progress! But nothing comes from nothing: the effect cannot contain more than the cause. What need to reason longer. The principle of causality imposes itself here with such stern evidence that it dispenses with all comment. To want to produce the greater from the less, that which is from that which is not, thought from matter, is to destroy this sovereign axiom; and to destroy the principle of causality is to cast one's self into the absurd—to upset reason itself. Is this the aim of Materialism? Let it declare it, then, and stand condemned. This triumph is too easy—I disdain it.

Let us concede to the Materialists that one can explain by mechanism the formation of all brute matter, give a reason for each simple body, its laws and infinite combinations, reduce it all to motion and superposition of motion; that the vegetable is but an admirable instrument, a pump acted upon by an invisible force to attract and reject the juices of which it is composed, a still constructed by an unequalled artist for the distillation of perfumes and essences. Is this enough? Concede even that the animal is a machine of a more complicated kind. Descartes has said so before them, Descartes, the proudest of metaphysicians, the master of philosophers.

Let us concede to the great geometrician, to the great mechanician, to the great psychologist, that those intelligent little dogs are but automatons obeying the pressure of a secret spring. You think, perhaps, brethren, that the Materialists will triumph, and that my concessions have put the truth in danger.

Reassure yourselves. If Science had reduced everything to mechanics, physics, and chemistry, if it had identified vegetable and animal life with the phenomena and forces of brute matter, if I wished to force Materialism into its last intrenchment, I have but to put this simple question: From whence does motion come? It will never answer. And had it by an impossibility found in matter the first cause of motion, it would suffice, to vanquish it, to make use of a simple thought, a single impulse of the will : I reason ; I love ; two words. This is not much ; but, nevertheless, it is enough to ruin the whole system of Materialism. I reason, I compare two ideas and seize their absolute connection ; I say, for example, Virtue is heroic ; martyrdom is a virtue, therefore martyrdom is heroic. It is very simple. Or again : Duty is the law of a free being ; it is before me ; I love it, and sacrifice all to it. Brethren, I appeal to you, from a mechanical movement, from any combination can you ever product duty and love ? Can you say seriously, as the Materialists do, Thought is a secretion of the brain, a result of the phosphorus with which that grey and white substance we carry under the cranium is impregnated ? What ! you make out thought to be the result of a merely mechanical motion ? But in order that it may be the product of such a principle, it must be of the same nature as it. Who will uphold this ? When I draw a conclusion do I perform an act of mechanism ? Do you hear the sound of the machinery ? have you instruments sufficiently delicate to reveal its internal tick tick ? When my will is bowed before duty, or is kindled by a violent love, do I act by machinery ? The saints, the grand geniuses, the heroes, are they all masterpieces of mechanism ?

Allow me to tell you, brethren, when one goes to the bottom of things, and grasps those doctrines which give themselves out as the pinnacle of Science, one pauses stupefied to find one's self face to face with absurdity, ashamed at being reduced to refuting principles whose mere enunciation is their peremptory condemnation!

How, brethren! it is necessary for me to establish that thought cannot result from mechanical, physical, or chemical matter? Why not? cry the Materialists; if thought were not the result of these combined forces, when the brain is less would thought be less? When the brain is troubled would thought be troubled? and when there is no phosphorus would thought be suppressed?

Brethren, but one word to refute this objection.

By what right does Materialism confound condition with cause? One, however, is distinct from the other. Condition has no direct influence on the phenomena which depend upon it. Cause, on the contrary, engenders them, produces them from itself. Air and a string in vibration are the conditions necessary to the sensible manifestation of harmony: the will is the cause. The brain is the condition of thought, not the cause. Does Materialism wish to prove the contrary? We are ready to hear it, and armed for reply with the principle of causality.

Moreover, if the soul were simply the result of the body and mechanical complications, it would depend totally and absolutely upon the body; why, then, does it so often subdue it? The body is exhausted: a prey to the fires of disease, you see it disorganize and die. If the soul is confounded with it, why does it seem to rise above this matter in ruins? Who has not felt it take the mastery and say to the body: "Fragile mechanism, yet one more effort, your master commands it. Your fibres are listless, your elasticity gone, but they shall yet vibrate once more." Who has not experienced this hour when, fully master of itself, the soul commands as sovereign its exhausted body?

I pity those who have not felt this, and I understand their being Materialists. But when one has had the upper hand, if but for a moment, of this rebellious matter, one becomes conscious of a force superior to it, which cannot be weighed in scales, which has nothing in common with physical or chemical energy, and which men have called by a name that expresses nothing material: one is conscious of one's soul, in fact.

The doctrinal work of Materialism is impossible, brethren. The pretension of explaining the entire creation by mechanism is laughable and senseless. But men do not start theories for the mere pleasure of so doing. One thinks to act, and to give to one's conduct a higher and more firm direction. If, then, one is a Materialist, it is not for the luxury of a witticism; it is, above all, to be able to live better. Let us see, then, the practical application of Materialism.

I stigmatize it as an immoral, despairing, and servile doctrine: immoral, as it breaks the spring of all progress; despairing, as it can do nothing to raise man crushed by trials; servile, as it engenders all social and individual oppression.

I would not on this point, brethren, force a conclusion. We priests are commonly reproached with always judging doctrines by their results, and thus preparing for ourselves an easy triumph. But in what respect is this tactic culpable? Guardians of every life willing to raise itself Godward, and of every conscience which will listen to Him, are we not obeying our divine mandate in forcing every word to say what it can do to moralize or corrupt man?

I do not pretend that every Materialist is immoral. Epicurus, the head of the school in antiquity, was remarkable for his moderation. That astonishes you. At the name of Epicurus, you picture a disordered soul eager for pleasure, a heart unbridled in its desires, exhausting to satiety the cup of intoxication. No, brethren, Epicurus, history relates, was temperate to refinement—less by virtue than by calculation. Man who enjoys without restraint, said he, is soon satiated; satiated, he is disgusted; disgusted, he despairs. And as a wise Materialist, Epicurus measured out his pleasure that the source might dry up less quickly, and remain more savoury. I do not give him to you as an example; I cite him merely as a proof that I do not ignore the calculated prudence of the Materialist, and do not make use of vain exaggerations to refute him.

Do you wish to touch with your finger the immorality of this theory? Put Materialism in the presence of man. Man longs to grow in life, for he is a progressive being. Now, to aid him in his magnificent evolution, what must be told him?

You must say to him, " Thou art free! Thou hast before thee both life and death, equal master of both. Wilt thou die? thou hast the pickaxe to break open thy tomb." " Man is in the hand of his counsel," says the book of God; "life and death are before him, and whether he liketh, shall be given him."

Ah! when this lesson is proclaimed to a people or a race; when you can implant in the heart of individuals and of nations the sentiment of liberty, you make of them laborious souls and proud natures, a people and a race of heroes, men of indefatigable energy, holding the sword well, not to oppress but to protect the weak, not to ravish the independence of others, but to preserve their own. They cannot be always victorious—victory is capricious—they are ever indomitable.

I would like to know the advice that Materialism gives to the young man, to the people, to a race—that which you teach, you doctors, I know too well. You preach the law of matter; you say to the young man, " the temperament is powerful!" Ah! he knows it as well as you. That which you say to a people I will tell you. You teach that matter has its laws! That which you say to the whole world, you sages! here it is without adornment: Matter! there is nothing but that. Matter! it is master. Matter! it is the God to be worshipped. And you think to make with such dogmas a free people, a generation of heroes, a new world! You deceive yourselves. Materialism gave its proof in Greece and Rome: to-day, as then, it will give birth to an enervated youth with no longer the figure for a soldier—it could not grow: which has no more blood in its veins—it has spent it: which has not the strength to raise a sword—it has neither muscle nor conviction.

Say that I lie! and prove to me that Materialism is not the supreme philosophy of degenerate peoples and worn-out races.

We must not only look, brethren, at man growing and prospering in life, we must look also at the feeble being destined to sorrow and trial. Destiny is stern with us, she has for us sorrows without name, and sufferings without number. Is there a single man who has not suffered? is there a woman who has not wept bitter tears? A young being who has not felt the disgust of life, and whose soul at the end of its strength has not cried out, "Who will console me?" is there one? Tell me. Are we not all broken and suffering? Who will console us? The earth? it is our martyrdom. Heaven? it is dark and obscure. What, then, your pleasures? They torture me. What will console me?

Answer, Materialists!

Ah! I know what you offer; you have given me intoxication—the intoxication which kills. And do you not see to-day how those console themselves who can live no longer? Do you not see where that crowd goes that the arrow of misery has wounded? Read the chronicle in the list of suicides!

God forbid that I should lay all these sinister

ends, these dark acts, upon the doctrine of Materialism. But you can well believe that when, armed with dagger or revolver, it sees nothing but matter, it is not God that speaks to this despairing generation. No, when to-day it dies, it is not God that kills it, and hangs the stone round its neck, that it may sink to the very bottom of the abyss. You have no consolation, and that is fatal. In these doctrines without a soul there is a despair without an end.

Would you measure, in social and political order, the vileness of this illiberal and heartless doctrine? Man is not born to live alone; he wishes to become a family and a nation. What are necessary to a family and a nation? Peace and liberty, fruits of virtue and justice and of love. What can Materialism give us? If the struggle for existence is the universal law, man is reduced to putting himself into antagonism with his fellow-men. Egotism becomes thus the first want and the first law; and the power of the State the only barrier to regulate and restrain it. Society is no longer a union of free beings, it is a group of slaves. By what right does Materialism dare to speak so much of liberty? Observe its current literature, and particularly the political literature; is it not in its mouth that the word liberty is always sounding? and yet it denies it. It is enough to shudder at! Sincerity before all! Away with liars and hypocrites. If you have suppressed a word in your schools, do not cry it in the public places.

Now, brethren, whether it will or no, Materialism

leads to servitude. And when you see rise up in a country these doctrines which recognize only the fatal laws of matter, and have room neither for the soul nor for liberty, that country is ripe for servitude and every oppression.

Ah, my brothers, it is not under Christ, under the Catholic faith, that nations are enslaved; it is not, as they are always saying, with a pope, even an infallible one, that consciences are enslaved. Their greatest act has been to free them, especially from the yoke of the Cæsars.

When you see on the contrary, Materialistic doctrines prevail, know that servitude is at hand and men are ripe for slavery. Cæsar approaches with measured steps, he glances round, his legions are on the alert, and before long you will be crushed beneath his spurred heels. When there is nothing but matter, there is but force, there are none but slaves; and, truly, why should you wish for liberty?

But I cannot predict for my country so sad a fate: France cannot be Materialistic. There is to-day a sort of fashion for Materialism; but, be assured, it is only on the surface. Would you know why this must be so? Because France is a country of clear ideas, where logic exists, a country where there is a heart.

Now Materialism is, as I have shown you, obscure in its principles; illogical in its deductions, as I have proved; and, as you have seen, without heart in its moral application as it is without consolation for practical life.

Whence have sprung these Materialistic ideas that eat into us? Why are they in our universities, our professions, our laboratories, and our amphitheatres? Why have the traditions of our great philosophers, of whom Descartes is the chief, been obscured and silenced? Why is the philosophy which looks upward, and speaks of the soul and the Infinite, silent before the philosophy which looks only on the ground and speaks to us of matter and its laws?

Plato leaves us, Epicurus returns; why?

Why, brethren?—I should not mix up in this place necessary truths with contingent facts. Yet let me—my faith and my patriotism cannot withhold it—let me tell you that the Materialistic ideas came from the other side of the Rhine something like twenty years ago, under the form of a mist which gilded the light of Science. They passed the stream, and our sky has become darkened and sombre.

We became no longer Catholics, we turned against our Church, we blushed for the old man who represents Christ amongst us. While losing our faith, we did not know how to keep our native intelligence. We said to this fog from the Rhine: " Come, and be our light ! "

And the fog has increased. It was welcomed by a great number of our savants. They said, " This comes from Germany; it is beautiful, it is true." It has penetrated our schools; it weighs upon our young generation like the lid of a tomb.

Brethren, the clouds came; and after them the

tempest of fire and sword. The clouds came first, the storm followed. Should I be very illogical if I had the audacity to tell you that the cloud was the beginning of the storm?

Well, turn, you who have certainly suffered by the storm of fire and sword, repulse the clouds, and hasten to conjure up a new tempest.

THIRD DISCOURSE.

ATHEISTIC PANTHEISM.

Brethren,
Error persists in closing to man all roads that lead him to the Infinite; and reason, which wishes to tread those paths in freedom, finds yet another system to conquer and to combat. It is not without grandeur nor attraction, and it knows how to mask with those qualities what it contains that is perfidious and disastrous. It is not narrow and exclusive, like positivism; or low and vulgar, like materialism. It does not proclaim like the one the superb pretension of correcting human nature—by mutilating it; it is far from the cynicism which by its strange worship of matter does not blush to lower us to the brute. It does not close, like the first, the doors of the Ideal; it throws them open: it does not, like the second, wish to reduce all to mechanism and geometry; it wishes life to be universal, and sees it everywhere. This is Pantheism.

But what, you will say, does not Pantheism affirm that all is God, or that God is everything? Then surely it is not an enemy, it is an ally.

Understand me: Pantheism has two decided and opposite forms; they arrive, I know, at the same result, but they go there by entirely contrary roads.

The essence of Pantheism is confusion, the substantial identification of the universe and God. The word itself indicates with precision this dogma: Πᾶν, all, the universe; Θεὸς, God. The universe is God. Now, there are two ways of obtaining this identification: one is to absorb the universe in God; it is thus formulated: God is the universe; the other is to confound God in the universe; it is thus formulated: The universe is God. One exaggerates God to the detriment of the world, the other exaggerates the world to the detriment of God. If one seems to strengthen Deism, the other is a declared atheism. "What do you seek for outside and above?" it cries. "There is nothing. God is not the transcendent law, He is the law emanating from things. The God you seek, insatiable minds, warped intelligences, is the universe itself; it is you. Let it suffice you!"

I will not stay to refute this first form of Pantheism. It is not to be feared, and it is not that which tends to prevail in this age. But if we have nothing to fear from mystic Pantheism we have all to dread from Atheistic Pantheism. That which is of import to our generation is not the religious inclination of souls athirst for God, it is the insatiable appetite of the earth. That which fascinates us is not the dazzling vision of heaven, but rather the dark mirage of matter. The sublime wanderings of mysticism do not trouble the soul of our contemporaries, and we are in no danger of being absorbed by those contemplative ones who, engrossed in God, see the world vanish before their dazzled eyes. No; the sect of Buddhists or Brahmins is in no danger of reviving, nothing is to be feared from their inoffensive doctrine. Why attack the dead? Let us respect their slumber, and let us leave in peace the great dreamers of India, China, Persia, and Egypt, the Pantheists of Greece, the Gnostics, the Neo-Platonists, the Mystics of the Middle Ages, the modern Pantheists of Germany. It is not a question of the parade of philosophic erudition; it is a question of attacking systems in vogue, which mislead minds and narrow souls by taking them from God.

Now, the living Pantheism of to-day is atheistic. It has made a redoubtable alliance with positivism and materialism, and these three dispute for our people. It speaks by the mouth of those who say, "Outside and above the universe there is nothing." It holds the pen of those who say, "God will always be the sum of the supra-sensible wants of the human soul; He is the category of the ideal."

It inspires those who reason: "God is the eternal to become, He *is* not—properly speaking, He is to be; God cannot exist; if the universe is, the perfect, or God, can but be conceived and dreamed of."

This it is which sings in those poems in which nature is deified, and where imagination given over to an idolatrous enthusiasm speaks to all that lives and breathes as one should speak to God alone. This it is which fears not to prefer to the true God, " This god, hazard and nature, which cannot be offended, which is *everything*, from the stone hidden in the bowels of the earth to the yellow mist which floats in a light cloud before the moon. This god which is breathed in with the air and the perfume of flowers, this god which is at once the water which flows and the wind which roars, the flower which opens to the sun and the sun which opens the flower, and the bee which buries itself in the flower's calix."

It is this Atheistic Pantheism in fine, which inspires our pagan morality, and deadens in corruption hearts vowed to the idolatry of themselves, deifying a matter that they should disdain.

I insist no further, brethren, I have said enough to show you the presence of the evil; henceforth it is our business to expose and conquer it.

What is the aim of a system, and the object of a theory? To explain that which is; consequently to determine the nature, principle, law, and end of things. Now, Atheistic Pantheism is completely summed up in four dogmas which contain the reply to these four fundamental questions.

There is but one substance and one being, substantial identification of God with the universe: first dogma.

At the origin, the beginning of things, there is the infinite, indeterminable, inconscient, impersonal in the power of being: second dogma.

The universe progresses and develops beneath the law of a blind and necessary progression: third dogma.

The final term of this progressive series, in incessant motion, is man: fourth dogma.

To refute these, is to sap the very foundations of Pantheism. Now, the first dogma goes directly to suppress the " I " and the divine personality; the second is a defiance of reason itself; the third is the total overthrow of conscience and liberty; the fourth, by leading to the deification of man on the ruins of God, of duty, and of liberty, leads to the deification of force, after engendering all servitude and fomenting all corruption. I will demonstrate this.

On your part, brethren, you whose personality is thus ignored, whose reason is insulted, and whose conscience is outraged by these false systems, may the just care for the future of that humanity, whose sons you are, teach you to unmask these baleful errors which cannot face the examination of a masculine intelligence, nor long captivate a sincere and prudent mind.

The very essence of Pantheism is the substantial identification of God and the universe; everything in this system tends to that end. Thus it is justly named the system of universal identity. There is but one substance, it says, one being; it is at the same time one and many, time and eternity, space and number, individuality and totality, principle, term and middle, infinite and finite, all in one.

Is this affirmation tenable? No, brethren, it is

a gratuitous postulate, having for its justification only, either an arbitrary definition of substance, or the difficulties presented by the substantial duality of the finite and the infinite. If, indeed, we defined substance, with Spinoza, as *that which is of itself*, one must logically infer the unity of substance; for God alone is of Himself, and the universe in connection with Him but a series of accidental and ephemeral manifestations. On the other hand, if to distinguish substantially the finite from the infinite, you expect to explain their co-existence and the mystery of creation, you would never free yourself from the theory of identity. But, first of all, the definition of Spinoza is contestable; then, with all those who take into account facts, I reply fearlessly: It is not possible to reduce the real and the ideal to identity.

Without doubt there exists a universal principle from which everything is derived, and to which all leads; but such an origin and end implies no confusion of substance between God and the universe. No doubt the divine idea, the Word—to speak in the language of Catholic doctrine—is the universal light, lightening all things with a ray of ineffable simplicity; but this light does not confound itself with the partial intelligences which emanate from it. It envelops without absorbing them. The suns which fill the universe and from which all light is derived, do they prevent the least spark from shining in our eyes? They make it pale, but they do not extinguish it.

It is a great and generous impulse, this tendency

of human intelligence towards unity, and it is not the least attraction of Pantheism that it promises us the satisfaction of the noblest and most imperious want of our reason.

Watch this exacting reason, follow it in its incessant activity, ask what it wants. You will find it seeking for the First Being which will enable it to bring together into one all the beings of creation; you will see it in search of that First Idea which will reveal in their simple clearness all inferior ideas. Is the ambition legitimate? is the dream realizable by merely human power? The Christian doctrine does not believe this.

The more the First Being is above our limited nature, the more the First Idea governs our confined intelligence. Left to himself man imagines the beginning of things, but he cannot reach it; he has a dim notion of the eternal light, but sees only its shadows and reflections; unity attracts him, but he is far from it, like those vessels at anchor in high sea, far from the coast that they can see but where they cannot land.

For man, and even for God Himself, unity will never be identity. On the one part, indeed, the beatific vision excludes all confusion of substance between ourselves and God; on the other, although all emanates from God, and God sees all in His unity, God remains substantially distinct from the beings that He has created, and that He moves by virtue of His word.

Would you have an irrefutable proof against the theory of identity? It is within us, in the very depths of our being, in the first word of conscience.

What is the "I"? The *I* is that which opposes the not *I*, that which can be no other. The "*I*" is indivisible, indestructible. Nothing has a hold on the "I." Matter is pulverized; to believe geometricians, the infinite is divisible: the "I" cannot be divided; it is that simple force which is confounded with nothing else, and against which nothing has any power. Like the atom, it is never lost; it can be but itself, and even the infinite cannot absorb it. Now, brethren, the "I" exists; your consciousness proclaims it, and was it but ever so little, that little would be sufficient to crush the theory of universal identity beyond all hope.

It is sufficient, in order to upset the scaffolding of doctrines in appearance the most learnedly established, to make use of one word, one fact, so long as the word is true, the fact undeniable. The word I oppose triumphantly to Pantheism is the word of Medea of old. "What remains to you?" they asked her. "Myself," she replied; "and it is enough."

Let us give ourselves the luxury of, I will not say a more complete, but a more extensive refutation; and prove to Pantheism that, like all false systems, it outrages the very reason it pretends to exalt.

What is the action of human intelligence? To know and to consider. It aspires to one first principle in order to discover the connection and the reason of things; it has not, however, as

Pantheism believes, the foolish pretension to confound and identify everything. It wishes to discover similitudes; but, at the same time, to recognize differences; the unity it seeks is one of harmony, not of substance.

Have you ever analyzed, my brethren, that which may be called the basis and foundation of the human mind? You discover in it four great immutable principles: the principle of identity, which serves to perceive similitudes; the principle of causality, which serves to make us grasp the origin of things; the principle of substance, which assists us in reducing the multiplicity of things to unity; the principle of contradiction, which obliges us to respect irreducible differences. The three first preside over the synthetic and unitive movement of our reason. The fourth governs this movement and moderates its tendency to unity.

To touch these principles is to violate reason itself, and to destroy them is to destroy it. Now, Pantheism is a deliberate attack against the principle of contradiction. In virtue of this axiom can we place under the same head the perfect and the imperfect, the yes and the no, the existent and non-existent? Can we identify two beings whose attributes are opposed? No, brethren, that is against common sense; it is a positive absurdity. Pantheism, by identifying God and the world, commits this absurdity. For instance: God is a perfect Being, or He is not. But this world which for the Pantheist is God, cannot be perfect, for it is ever changing. All in it moves; nothing is stationary, all progresses. Matter transforms itself; minerals balance by hidden movement their invisible atoms; the planets roll in their immense orbits, without repose or cessation; they moved yesterday and will move to-morrow. Whither do they go, and what do they seek? Who can tell? This only is certain, they do go and they do seek. Life is in unquiet labour, never satisfied, never fatigued.

And man? What moving activity! what absorptions! what alternations of mistakes and hopes, of happiness and anguish! What a fever of life! what a breathless race along this road without an end, which opens to his ambition an indefinite progress! "The whole creation groaneth and travaileth in pain together until now."

Well, my brethren, what does all this movement prove? It condemns the doctrine of Pantheism. Do you not see that that which moves seeks something; that which seeks something is wanting in what it seeks; that which is wanting, were it only in an atom, is not perfect? Thus, here is contradiction between the perfect and the imperfect. To identify them would be to destroy one of the first principles of reason. Let Pantheism, if it will, accomplish this impious and illogical work, we will keep our intelligence whole, our identity inviolable; and in the name of reason this identity will proclaim the irreducibility of the imperfect, which is the universe, and the perfect, which is God, into the same substance.

God being suppressed by this sacrilegious confusion, what remains to the origin of your deified universe? Let us ask Pantheism. The Infinite. The Infinite? That is the reply of the Catholic doctrine. We also place the Infinite at the beginning of things; only we differ in two important points from the system of identity.

To begin with, for us the Infinite is not, as Pantheism teaches, a force *emanating* from things, it is a transcendent force. It contains the universe, and consequently is present to the universe; but the universe does not contain it, and consequently it transcends the universe. More: for us this Infinite is identical with perfection; for Pantheism it is but a *to be*, undeterminate, impersonal, inconscient, a sort of nameless chaos, which is more than nothing and is not yet something.

Here the doctrine we are attacking enters into a path without issue; it will not be difficult to master and reduce it.

Why should we place an Infinite at the base and origin of things, in order to account to ourselves for the phenomena whose yearly unfolding forms the drama of creation? With all its Infinite can Pantheism do so? It pretends it can, but falsely; and as, to sustain its "universal identity," it has had to tread underfoot the principle of contradiction and condemn itself to an absurdity, so, to defend its strange and false "Infinite," it will be obliged to upset another principle of reason and condemn itself a second time to an absurdity.

What, indeed, can you ever produce from the

indeterminate, the inconscient, from blind force? What! the universe, with its innumerable forms, whose variety and contrast increase their harmony; the universe, that you see gradually emerging from chaos, progressing from mechanism into life, from insensible life to sensible life, from sensible life to conscious, free, and intelligent life—that universe the produce of your pretended Infinite? That which, according to you, has no being, as it is but a power which is to be; and that which has no order, as it is but a blind force; that which has neither life, consciousness, nor freedom, as it finds life only in man—that intangible Infinite, can it have produced all things? My brethren, to sustain such a paradox one must abdicate one's very reason!

And the principle of causality, the principle of satisfied reason, the principle of determinateness, that invincible axiom which shows us in facts that only which is in the cause—what will you do with it? Can you ever reconcile it with your doctrine? It is impossible to banish it; submit to it, then, and renounce these untenable theories.

These sophists, brethren, do not recoil at this; and you are face to face with men who dare to proclaim, to the contempt of all common sense, the identity of yes and no, of being and of nothingness, as the acme of enfranchised reason and the philosophy of the future!

How can such assertions be defended? how could that inexplicable German Algebra of Hézel's ever have been formulated? you ask me, brethren. Here is the key; I am very glad to give it you, and to introduce you into this foggy land in order to bring some light into it.

The famous principle of the identity of existence and non-existence, from whence has issued the logical identity of contradictions, comes from that false Infinite which Pantheists have put at the origin of all things. In it, certainly, being and not-being are confounded. It is not, strictly speaking, because it is to be; it is, however, because from it all things come. Thus, the sophists conclude triumphantly, in the eyes of a clear reason which has reached the absolute principle of things, contraries are identified. For the profane there still exists a difference between yes and no, between existence and non-existence; but to the initiated sage all difference is effaced—he is in the full sunlight of identity.

These clouds were the rage on the other side of the Rhine. The mania was such that Germany was too narrow to contain it; and France, degraded and forgetful of her genius, made herself the complaisant assistant of her dark and terrible neighbour.

These formulas which overthrow reason to attack God are applauded. All, certainly, in this country have not countenanced these blasphemies, but too great a number have received them. Doubtless in questions of doctrine there is no nationality; but believe me, brethren, if truth knows no country and owns no frontier, error does.

Let us not, then, accept these poisonous products of foreign importation; and should only two hands be raised to applaud them, two hands would be too many: patriotism alone, in default of logic, should command silence.

Do not be astonished, brethren, that these subtle and complicated doctrines, so carefully erected, can be refuted by the first principles of reason, by those simple truths which illumine every soul that comes into the world. Error is less difficult to conquer than you think. It seeks to impose upon you with an air of daring and security; this is merely a tactic. All that is false is fragile. The truth alone is invincible. Error, whether giant or colossus, is easy to break and overturn. Giant, its name is Goliath; it is aggressive like the Philistine, but the shepherd's sling is sufficient to destroy it. There needs, to slay it, but one stone from the side of the mountain. The stone of the sling, brethren, you all possess in those immortal axioms that are your very reason itself. The mountain is God. And if savants, unnatural thinkers betraying their own genius, rebel against reason and against God; if, in contempt of this very reason and of the God from whom it came, they remain obstinate in their vain and false systems—well, then I will appeal to the people; I will have recourse to the reason of the masses: and it is from the crowd of simple and honest ones that that David will arise, armed, to strike on the head these false giants who prostitute their strength to insult the people of God.

And progress, brethren—that progress of which the Pantheists make such a grand parade, which they proclaim as the universal law of things, as the very life of their deified cosmos—that progress whose development they follow with their science, and that they even sing of in their enthusiastic poetry;—what can we say to this? Here, at least, is Pantheism true? At first sight nothing more beautiful or more indisputable. Nothing more beautiful; for all that grows and develops impresses you with indescribable life and splendour. Nothing more indisputable; for if there is a phenomenon which must strike every eye, it is the harmonious and progressive movement of the universe.

Question the heavens: astronomy will tell you the history of those luminous giants which an invisible Hand has cast into space without limit, and which move on their fiery tracks. How surely they advance, how harmoniously they group themselves! It is not a rabble cast hither and thither, rushing madly about in space; it is an army marvellously organized, whose bewildering evolutions are regulated without faltering or error by an unseen and inexorable force. Never does the smallest planet stray. The most erratic comets follow to a hair the line that has been assigned to them—by whom? you ask the Pantheist. What does that matter? he replies; it has but one road to go. Progress is blind, and therefore single.

Remember this, brethren; it is important. Let us meanwhile pursue a little further this living and admirable law of progress, this ever-changing earth that we tread underfoot.

The crust of this planet might appear to you overthrown by the influence of strange and unknown disturbing forces: but no, nothing is disorderly in the universe; disturbance exists only to those incapable of grasping the general order of things. All is in its place. The very volcanoes are as measured in their violent eruptions as the quiet flowers open to the rays of the sun. Nothing which is could be otherwise than as it is. All moves, but without ever losing the place assigned to it. No exception to the law. Life seems to escape it; no, brethren, that which we call its caprice forms an admirable epic whose every scene and act is prearranged. Flowers have their regular development like the constellations of heaven. Trees and giant oaks are like a nation whose boundary has its strict inviolable laws. Well, and then? Then, you see, says the Pantheist, progress declares itself in higher stages, and is superposed with invariable regularity. No creature escapes this inevitable action, and man himself consummates it without modifying the law. He is the last product of the evolution of the eternal " to be," that Infinite whose inexhaustible depth knows no sterility, and engenders in spite of itself all that it evolves. Then all is necessary in this forced progress of things? Certainly, that which comes from the Infinite cannot issue otherwise than as experience has proved it. That which is must be. How? Must humanity itself bow to the law of fate? Yes, everything is fatal. But is not man free? Has he not a conscience which asserts the distinction between good and evil? If evil exists there are surely things which should not be, for evil is exactly that which ought not to be; and then, in the face of liberty of conscience, and of evil, what becomes of your law of progress?

Yes, my brethren, if all should obey, if all in heaven and earth should bear witness to the exclusive law imagined by Pantheism, a terrible power, liberty, would be sufficient to confound it. If every planet and every star is held subject, man is not. He is free. He can do wrong: he can violate the law; he can go astray; his power to do evil and his very falls prove that all is not subject to an inexorable Fate—they demonstrate that the law of progress as understood by Pantheism is false and immoral. Choose, then, between that moral consciousness which infallibly teaches good and evil, and that doctrine which by suppressing all distinction between good and evil ruins the very basis of conscience, and confounds vice and virtue as it does yes and no, existence and non-existence.

You will respect, I am convinced, liberty and conscience, and you will retain virtue, which is more valuable than a host of brilliant sophisms. A system which finds no place for it has none, either, for truth: goodness is the touchstone of truth.

Therefore, brethren, behold the universality of things according to Pantheism in full bloom. The great All is raised little by little, step by step; the pyramid is constructed on the vast foundation of the Infinite; it terminates in man, who is the crest and crowning point of all. Man! this is the end of all things. The thinking, conscient being; such is the last limit of this irresistible *processus*.

Upon what is this assertive doctrine founded? Is it not, to say the least, rash—certainly hypothetical—to assign, as limit to the evolution of universal life, man, who covers with misery, as well as grandeur, that world on which for a moment he breathes, vegetates, and dies? Has the impersonal and inconscient Infinite of the Pantheists confided to them his secret? But truly, if he has done so much, why does he not do more? How! it is on this grain of sand called a planet, it is in human thought, that doubtful light, it is in the dispersed and devouring race of the sons of man, that he exhausts his irresistible and incommensurable fecundity!

I will not stay to consider that which is arbitrary and gratuitous in its doctrine of the finality of things. A startling problem arises: what will Pantheism do with man, whom it proclaims as the highest form of the progress of things?

What will it do? It will deify him.

Always the same conclusion. When one enters into these radical errors of positivism, materialism, or Pantheism, one begins by denying God, one ends by deifying man.

A God! They must always have a God! The true cast away, they turn to some idol, and raise up altars to a vain image, like the Israelites of old.

But what is this God of yours, you idolaters? The most refined, taking what is sublime in him—thought—called it the Ideal. What! the living God to whom I pray, whom I adore, whom I have so often invoked in my misery with a broken heart —this God is the mere idea of man's brain! Yes; for all reality is poor and imperfect; the perfect can only be a conception of reason. What? That which humanity has loved, that it has sang of through centuries, that whose voice it thought itself to have heard, whom it believed itself to have seen in Christ—that God was but a deceitful mirage of reason,—that deluded reason which naïvely embodied its own visions! But this is sad even to bitterness, and afflicting even to despair! Thus logic wills; thus an inexorable Science exacts! O savant, keep your logic and your science, keep that which you call strict truth! Your science is false, your logic blind, your truth a lie, since they lead to these ghastly results. Where despair is there can never be truth.

More positive in their Pantheism, others, well knowing that humanity cannot be satisfied with abstract ideas and fanciful dreams, deify real humanity.

Take care, then, for a terrible abyss will open. From the time that humanity is the supreme force of things, you must submit to the pressure of numbers, the tyranny of force, the despotism of intelligence. You must re-establish in the human reign that law which spread and prevailed in the darkest ages. Now, in the darkest ages, who governed? The strongest. Who was in the right? The strongest. Who existed on the ruin of others? The strongest; sometimes the luckiest.

It will be the same in humanity; and the strongest in humanity is the mass. The strongest is the most intelligent and the most able. How, brethren, you would consent to deify thus strength and the mass, ability and even reason? But if the mass goes astray, if reason wanders? Do we not see every day how weak and inconstant the mass of humanity is? A word rouses them into fury; a word appeases them. A caprice renders them infatuated with liberty; a panic disconcerts them, and casts them at the feet of a Cæsar. Is that what you would deify! But reason? It is no more sure. What temptations are there not to the greatest minds! what dreams of ambition, of tyranny, and of egotism! What inflames the world? What sets at war nations and races? What lets loose the most implacable scourge upon this planet? Is it not intelligence become the accomplice of ambition and passion? There remains only the weak, the poor, virtuous souls and honest hearts, gentle to others, stern only with themselves. What place shall they have in this barbarous system which deifies what it should rather scourge? If you must sacrifice any, sacrifice rather the wicked —not the righteous, not the self-denying. But in deified humanity it cannot be so; the last word will ever remain to the strongest, without appeal. To what will you have recourse against this God? To heaven? It is empty. To earth? It belongs to the most powerful. To right? It is no longer more than the expression of force. Force alone speaks in this nation of slaves.

And this is the conclusion to which Pantheism inevitably leads. It destroys God by sacrificing man; after sacrificing man, it brings him to despair; after bringing him to despair, it degrades him. What a prospect!

Ah! my brothers, it is not thus in the Christian world, in the humanity that Christ purchased with His blood, enlightened with His wisdom, transformed with His Spirit. Those will there be crowned who, without having had genius, strength, or fortune—which depends on no one,—have had—that which depends upon ourselves—virtue. And He, the crucified God, wills to appear to man, His brow encircled with the glory of the righteous, the meek-spirited, the self-denying of this world.

If Jesus Christ was not God, He would be the greatest and best of all that have ever trod this earth. To Him will turn all those who put love and goodness above genius and power, those who would subdue might to right, and man to God.

FOURTH DISCOURSE.

SCEPTICISM.

BRETHREN,

Certain men dare to assert that souls have no life; that they simply vegetate. You see crowds of men of pleasure, men of art, men of interest; but *men*, where are they to be found? The excessive development of material civilization has precipitated the abasement of moral life, and the abasement of moral life has provoked a more disastrous invasion than that of foreign armies, the invasion of philosophical and religious Scepticism. Hence a dearth of men.

Scepticism prevents their growth, and kills them in the germ.

Nowadays, my brethren, people believe the truths demonstrated by experimental Science, but not those which go beyond it. They believe those truths deduced by simple logic, but not those proclaimed by revelation; they believe in everything that can be felt, weighed, or measured, but in nothing which is beyond the material proof of the senses.

They believe in matter, they doubt the soul;

they believe the phenomena which speak of the laws of the universe, they doubt God who made the universe; they believe in the fatality of matter, they doubt that liberty which is the law of intelligence; they believe all that is lower than man, they doubt all that is within and above him. They believe in the life which passes, because man dies; they do not believe in the life which passes not, and which alone can give to the soul, freed from earthly dust, the full satisfaction of its longings. They believe in pleasures and seek to live in them; they believe in interest, and make it their god; they do not believe in virtue. They believe in appearances, but not in realities. They believe in that which is played upon the stage, but not in that genius which manages the stage and influences the players.

Faith, which has been the life of past ages, which is found in the cradle of every nation, inspiring its virtues and watching over its destiny—that faith we lack; the fountain is as it were dried up.

Souls are in despair; families are dissolved, the hearths are cold, the people are unquiet; races deteriorate; a dull anguish weighs down this generation bitten by doubt. No more enthusiasm, no more hope, no future. A whole cycle has passed; and the pale survivors of that cycle, worn out, seem anxious for death. We are sad, very sad, whatever they may say. Noisy pleasures can only deceive those who do not look below the surface. In the very depths there is a well of anguish, a world of agony.

Shall we then die? No, we will not die! Let those who will, do so! Let those who have renounced all hope, die! Did I come to prophesy the end of all things, you would protest, you would silence me, young souls full of life, who are the seeds of a brighter future; mothers who look upon your sons with eyes of hope, and see in them the intrepid heroes of your dreams; you all, who cannot believe that the world has spoken its last words, and for whom faith remains still the principle of all that consoles, regenerates, and exalts our humanity.

Then this question arises, inevitably and imperiously: As, to live, one must believe, what is necessary to make us believe? I reply, It is necessary to kill Scepticism, and, to kill, it is necessary to know it.

What, then, is this Scepticism. What is its strength? How has it corrupted us, and by what means can it be destroyed?

Scepticism is the abnormal, unhealthy doubt of intelligence. I say abnormal and unhealthy, as there is a doubt which is both healthy and legitimate. Before a clearly perceived truth reason assents; before a plainly demonstrated error it recoils and dissents. But if it does not clearly perceive either truth or error, it hesitates between assent and denial: this is the wise and reflective doubt, and the path which leads to truth. Far from being an evil, this state is an intellectual virtue. If we know how to doubt wisely, we shall be less easily carried away by false doctrines, and will often avoid many irreparable misfortunes.

In what, then, does the unhealthy, illegitimate doubt of reason consist? In that it refuses to adhere to that which is duly demonstrated, and takes no measures to quit uncertainty, which is a passing state, to enter into conviction, which is the definite and obligatory state of the intelligence with regard to Truth. Scepticism is of two kinds: one systematic and considered, the other unconsidered and unconscious.

I will interrogate the first upon the great moral and religious questions. "What do you think of the spirituality of the soul?" "According to some the soul is spiritual, according to others it is only matter; for my part, I don't know." "And immortality?" "Some affirm that the soul exists after death, others that it is annihilated; for my part, I don't know." "And providence?" "According to some it rules over all, according to others everything is false; for my part, I don't know."

These are those who, without following the school of any philosopher, hesitate perplexed before these great truths; they all suffer from doubt, more or less reflective, not formulated into a system.

Beside these are philosophers who say, "Man sees things as they appear to him, not as they are. Ideas are forms of the intellect. To seize the truth it must be proved that ideas are the exact image of the objective reality; such a proof is impossible." Thus, after having daringly fathomed the very depths of reason, they suspect its legitimacy; and instead of recognizing as true that which it demonstrates, they rebel against it, repeating the words

K

of Brutus to Virtue: "Reason, thou art but a name!"

Is Scepticism actually present in modern society? Is it a superannuated doctrine like alchemy or the astronomy of Ptolemy, or a living doctrine, governing and seducing men's minds?

Of all errors it is, to my thinking, the most widespread, the most blindly obeyed, and the most sadly influential. Scepticism possesses a public school and a public instruction; consequently it is armed with the two greatest forces an idea can make use of to subjugate men's souls.

You are astonished, brethren. You ask me where it is taught, where it is proclaimed; you possibly think it out of date, like Kant and his philosophy? No: doubt, religious and philosophical, always exists; its name only is altered. It hides itself under a new title full of prestige; it calls itself positivism.

What does it do, then? Does it deny matter? On the contrary, it openly professes its worship, and has the pretension to know it more completely than any one has known it before. There is the secret of its influence and its triumphs in this age athirst for matter, and whose supreme ambition is to move, transform, and vanquish it. Thus, what does positivism say? "Matter alone exists, it is everything to man. When you know it and its forces, you will be masters of the world; nothing henceforth will resist you. You must seek for nothing outside matter. It alone is certain; the rest is a dream. All which concerns the soul or that which is called God, all which makes the domain of philosophy and religion, must be considered out of date by the positive reason of this age; it is a nightmare which our awakened minds must at length shake off."

Know, then, my brethren, if there is a doctrine well followed in this our day, it is that. I say to believers tranquil in their Church, sleeping in their faith, " Undeceive yourselves; it is not your *Credo* that will enlighten and direct this lost world, this society adrift." I say to the spiritualists, who believe in the persistency of their action, " Your reign is over!" I say even to the materialists, persuaded that their coarse and noisy declarations will influence humanity, " No, you are not masters. The error which threatens the future, and which sways young and educated minds, is positivism. It holds a school and an almost popular tone of thought; and it knows how, with treacherous art, to disguise its doubts and its denials under the ardent worship of Science, its material certainties and its useful application." Let those whose troubled hearts interrogate with so much anguish the destiny of humanity, and who believe that with sterile regrets they can preserve the world from threatened misfortune, know this.

You will answer, " Is not this doctrine as good as another? Well, then, doctrine for doctrine, if this is the time for a rejuvenated Scepticism, let it reign. Revelation has had its day, spiritualism its day; make room for the new-comer, the hour has arrived of a more perfect civilization." Impossible, my brethren. There can never be room for Scepticism, for it is the destruction and ruin of all moral life; it can only establish itself on corruption and reign over the grave.

Moral life consists in the amelioration of one's self: therein is its very essence. It rests upon conviction: therein is the guarantee of its efficacy. To make myself better, I must believe in good—in the obligation which binds me to it; I must believe in my soul—in a principle distinct from matter. I must also believe in my free will, in my responsibility; for if I am not free and responsible I cannot dispose of myself, I cannot lead myself to good and fly from evil. I must believe not only in the useful, of which I cannot deprive myself without suffering; in the pleasant, of which I cannot deprive myself without sacrifice; in the necessary, of which I cannot deprive myself without peril; but I must also believe in virtue, that is in goodness, from which I cannot free myself without cowardice and disgrace. I must believe that the heroes of duty were not fools, nor duty an illusion; and if I leave this world butchered by a republican, or crushed by a tyrant, I must leave it with a glad heart and a serene mind, convinced that all those who have lived, those who have suffered, and those who have made others suffer, the executioner and the victim, will pass before an avenging and incorruptible law. I must believe in the eternal balance which weighs justly the virtues, sacrifices, and martyrdoms of living souls.

If Scepticism upsets beliefs, how can the moral life subsist? If it shatters them without mercy, is it possible that the righteous man, the man who struggles against himself, who is utterly devoted, who does not calculate before everything his interest and his pleasures, but who ever places first honesty, justice, and self-abnegation—is it possible that this man, I say, can exist? No, my brethren; all those who are at war with virtue are void of conviction, and all those who strive after good look towards God and eternity. The mainspring of virtue is beyond the grave.

What remains to thee, sceptic? Thou hast overturned all; matter alone has found favour. But, great God! what is there in this matter? Pleasure; interest; it is a strange fairy, who has but to stretch out her wand and it distils ecstasy and changes all to gold. And the laws of matter? The laws of matter may be summed up in a word that gives a shudder when one feels one's self proud and independent—a word that you, perhaps, all know: force! Pleasure, interest, force! This is the trinity which is put in place of that one which is called Sovereign Intelligence, Infinite Love, Illimitable Power! And that is the corner-stone upon which they pretend to found Science, and to establish the future world. The future world is too large to rest upon this grain of sand; too big to be supported on this atom! Turn and twist matter as you may, analyze it and combine it as much as you will, you will never find more than the atom. Now the atom, with its three attributes, pleasure, force, and interest—what is it in the presence of moral life? Pleasure! I am obliged to tread it underfoot; for moral life consists in immolating one's self to duty: when one is a man of pleasure, one cannot be a man of virtue. Interest! I must sacrifice it at once to something which is dominant over all else: honesty. Force! There is a superior law—right—before which it must bend itself. If, unfortunately, I do not recognize above force another power, which is called liberty, it is finished. Moral law is henceforward a vain word, and the human world, like the other inferior ones, has only to submit, crushed, to a blind, inexorable, and despairing law: fatality.

Let us fly this Scepticism which undermines us. Let us tear ourselves away from the deathly grasp of pleasure, interest, and force; if not, we are lost. Pleasure penetrates into our very fibre, bringing with it a host of dishonouring vices, driving before it generations wasted to the very marrow, who can but disappear, since they have no longer enough blood to make them worthy to live. Interest goes before aught else; the race of egotists ready to devour each other increases. Force prevails over conscience and liberty; we shall soon be but a nation of slaves, understanding, perhaps, but too late that liberty no longer exists, and that she has left us at the same time as the Gospel.

The corrosive power of Scepticism is exercised not only against the mind; it directly attacks the will, the very agent of moral life.

If intelligence perceives what is good, the will

SCEPTICISM.

performs it. If intelligence is the light of life, will is its strength. Strange fact, in spite of the mysterious correlation between these two faculties, there yet exists a certain independence between them. One may be a genius, yet not possess a strong will; unless one has a mind capable of strong convictions, no strength of will can exist. You find in history men of admirable intelligence, yet with hearts of ice. Weigh the energy of their will: it is almost null; they are merely contemplative, and live only with their brain. Look at what we call a sectarian, that man of action, the propagandist who strives to rally proselytes round his idea and make it a banner. You will not find a large cranium—the sectarian has a narrow head—but always a mind that grasps firmly, as the anchor does the rock, and will not let go.

Those men who have accomplished great things, who by means of an overpowering idea have stirred nations and worlds—great legislators and great captains, heads of states and great reformers—all have been armed with invincible convictions. Also, my brethren, when a doctrine shakes the mind's conviction, it enervates by consequence the moral force and will which animate it. Now, it is the very essence of Scepticism to ruin every conviction of the mind, to strike the rock of our thought and reduce it to powder. And for that reason one sees nowadays, under this reign of doubt and under the influence of a thousand doctrines before whose wind all is carried away, wills enervated and characters rendered weak.

How little energy and determination there is! how little vigour and spontaneity! You see everywhere souls ready to bend and be governed; you find scarcely anywhere free and independent souls. The spirit of rebellion, which has breathed over the masses, has emancipated nothing; it has only multiplied slavery under the lying title of liberty. When one is independent, one remains an individual; one does not become a vile unit in an army of serfs. Individualities disappear; herds increase. Look at France; a mountain yesterday, to-day she is but a shifting sand moved by the storm. Scepticism has pulverized her. It has reduced to nothingness this nation which was great, this generation which was powerful, this race which had a name, and which, if it does not take care, may perhaps to-morrow have none. There was once love, there is now reviling; there were brothers, and there are now enemies. There were men there once; there are now only corpses, skeletons that are moved, and, striking against each other, break like rotten bones.

Scepticism is like a disease of the brain: it is incurable. One is cured of the fever of pleasure which attracts youth; one is cured of ambition, of a foolish love for things of the earth; one can be cured of every passion and every vice. But when religious and philosophic doubt, sown in the soul, has grown and achieved its ruin, the man is mortally attacked, and he dies. Christ alone can breathe upon these dead souls and revive them. Therefore do I understand the cry of the Apostles,

"Lord, increase our Faith." To believe is a gift of God. To believe after having doubted is a miracle of His providence.

Our age is carried away by philosophic and religious doubt; must we then despair? No; for God watches over us, and Scepticism has not invaded everything. If there are souls deeply contaminated by doubt, others are not so, and ask no better than to believe. These souls we both can and ought to preserve. To do so it is necessary to know how in this epoch doubt spreads in men's minds.

This contagion arises, first of all, from that systematic and exclusive instruction which limits itself to the science of matter, and which passes over the science of God and the soul.

The instruction given, whether to the people or to the educated classes, is radically insufficient. The total domain of intelligence comprises three regions: the region of matter, the region of the soul, the region of God. Now, on the very strength of the institution which governs us, and of the routine to which we are bound, the young are merely taught the sciences of matter. All that concerns the soul, all that touches upon God, is systematically put aside and finally despised. How can doubt do otherwise than creep in here? Not to doubt one must adhere to the truth; to adhere to the truth one must know it. If you are not taught it, you cannot know it; if you do not know it, you cannot adhere to it. As all philosophy is proscribed and theological science forbidden, as they neglect the synthesis of human knowledge, you are condemned to believe only in the world of matter, to ignore the things of the soul and the mysteries of God, consequently to doubt them.

You make mathematicians—they are, I admit, first-rate ones—you produce men of science, and Europe envies you them; you make men that you think great because they can quell insurrections; but you do not train the master minds that can prevent them; and, besides, that which you do *not* produce—and it is what we want before everything—is a *thorough man*,—a man of scientific, philosophical, and religious thought: a man whom the earth obeys, because his science has mastered it; whom the people listen to, because he understands the laws of humanity; and whom God blesses, because he remains the servant of God.

Those who are called to direct the world and to govern come from a school which turns out savants, no longer from the system which produces thinkers. What has become of this system? It existed at the time when our greatest geniuses flourished. Then we saw them in the name of one powerful idea shake, overthrow, and regenerate nations. But to-day religious thought is veiled and philosophy seems crushed; scarcely have we any philosophers or any theologians; statesmen have passed away; we have only business men left, and they do not see far enough to see justly; therefore the world, deprived of its guides, turns to Scepticism, tired of groping for its road in the dark.

Beware, brethren, lest this increasing Scepticism prepares dark days for us. When the heavens are hid I feel afraid, for the night is at hand. And when night falls, you approach the rocks without seeing them! They see you, imprudent navigator, and draw on your heedless ship. You jest to-day, in spite of danger, careless and light-hearted; take heed, to-morrow you may strike upon the rock and sink.

The number of attacks, of which religion and philosophy are the objects, also serve to nourish Scepticism.

Observe, brethren—I wish to impress it upon you—we do not fear war. We do not ask that those who do not think as we do should be gagged. It would be neither wise nor humane. Moreover, however strong the gag we would use to stifle error, it would soon be broken. Repression soon wearies; false doctrines, exasperated but not vanquished, explode, and their explosion is often the more terrible, the more violent the restraint has been.

This remark made, I resume. The attacks on philosophic and religious truth are universal in this age, and its chief characteristic. Not a day nor an hour passes without reason or faith having to suffer some brutal and subtle aggression. There exists in the world a powerful machine which knows no rest. It rolls on without ever tiring, like a steam engine, more noisy and indefatigable than the waves of the sea; that is the press. Ask what this civilized world does. I can reply: it prints. All its life is taken up with writing, talking, or reading. Well! look into what it prints; you will see at the bottom of everything, of literature, history, politics, science, and philosophy, of all serious ideas as of all frivolous ones, some hit at the truths of philosophy and religion.

In other days the attack was confined to a laboratory, an amphitheatre, an academy, or the chamber of a savant; to-day, it is everywhere. It taints the child at school, the man in the workshop, the woman in the drawing-room or at the hearth, and the speaker in the public place. Every truth is denied. God is no more than a dream; the soul, a myth; liberty, an illusion; Providence, the law of fate; the Church, a human institution; revelation, a mere phenomenon of the conscience; Christ, a philosopher and a great man. Never before in any age or nation has such a tempest assailed truth. All is shaken. Conviction falters—what do I say? it is a phenomenon as rare as the antediluvian beasts. You still see erudite men, but you scarcely find men of conviction.

You live in tranquillity, you happy believers, kneeling in your churches with hands upraised to heaven; you enjoy divine consolations; you pray for the world, and have no idea that a horrible tempest is passing over it, breaking down, overthrowing, and devastating everything! Whilst calm reigns, the sun shines and there is not a breath of air, and the very leaves of the trees are motionless. I understand this inaction. But when the tempest of doctrine roars and the whole land shakes, it is useless to close our eyes; these clamours strike us, and these shocks disturb us in spite of ourselves. It is no longer enough to pray; we must fight. You must rouse the sleeping Lord, and force Him to interfere in the might of His arm to save those that are dying. Arise and gird up your loins; now is the hour for the great battle of God!

Brethren, there is a third cause of Scepticism. I feel in speaking of it a certain amount of reluctance, yet truth compels me, and I must bear it witness. Shall I hurt any one here by recognizing that the reply to the universal objections raised against our faith is insufficient? I do not say insufficient in itself; truth can fear nothing, either from the objection or from those who advance it. Truth is immutable; whatever is said, whatever is done, truth remains. But it may happen that, by the fault of the age and the inferiority of the men, truth, in itself irresistible, has not all the radiancy that it should have, nor all the triumph which is its due.

Well, in my reserve and in my sincerity, after the experience that I have had of the sceptics and the sick souls of this day, after the work which Divine Providence has given me for the maintenance of the truth, I do not fear to recognize the fact that the reply and the defence is not always equal to the attack and the difficulty.

That is why, young people, you are vanquished. That is why you who live in your age, astounded at all that Science parades before you, sincere intelligences eager for the truth—that is why you cannot grasp it; that is why you are a prey to doubt, and oscillate like an edifice shaken by the wind, whose unsteady columns quiver and menace ruin.

Is it that God has left us? God leaves no one. A loyal soul will ever find that which can enlighten it, always the book of life, always the man of God to interpret it. Trust is in the power of the whole world, and that leads to Faith.

What is it necessary to know in order to reply victoriously to Science and Philosophy? The man who wishes to master those who attack him, and keep proudly and faithfully his chiefest good—Faith; the man who will not flee from the battle-field, or entrench himself in an easy disdain, in a politic and pusillanimous evasion; the man who wishes to say, "I believe, and I know why I believe;" the man who wishes to preserve this victorious attitude;—this man must know that Science and that philosophy in whose name he is attacked, and put them in accordance with the faith they honour.

No one will be sufficient for this labour, say the timid. No one? This is an insult to human intelligence, a want of respect for reason, for Faith, and for the God who has made us men! To reign must Faith run away? To believe must intelligence veil its eyes? Well, I tell you that Faith should reign in the world of Science; I tell you that she should enter into the laboratories and amphi-theatres, wherever Science works, in order to complete it by imparting to it her divine light. And know well that we have nothing to fear from Science and from the thousand obstacles that are raised in its name. But to show that we are invincible against it, we must know it like those who practise it, and not desert the battlefield and refuse the combat. We must reunite in the whole synthesis Science and Faith, and prove by its very example that if Science illuminates the earth on which we are held captive, Science and Faith, mingling together their rays, can alone illumine and penetrate into the heavens to which all our thoughts and aspirations are turned. How shall we keep from doubt those minds that it threatens? This is the question to solve. The work is difficult, but necessary.

And, first of all, my brethren, you who have the forms of your belief, remember that Faith is not to be defended by either abuse, violence, or passion. Abuse? They will abuse you more cruelly. Violence? They will oppose worse. Passion? It never yet proved anything. The old proverb is well spoken, "Those who are angry are in the wrong." Nothing is calmer than Right. A man on the side of truth never lets himself be troubled by anger; the tranquil genius is that most inspired by religious faith. Look at Saint Thomas Aquinas. When you look into the deep thoughts of this man, they seem to you like those super-terrestrial regions where the air currents can still be felt, but where tempests cannot reach. Look into inferior souls: there the volcano rumbles; and in the scarcely formed earth, you feel each disturbance and hear each groan of misery, sad attribute of earthly being. Would you master those who attack you? You must do this; learn and arm yourself. Learn those religious and philosophic truths which you ignore; arm and fit yourself for war by taking, not a material sword, but the sword of the Spirit; for the Spirit of God has its own sword and its own armour.

Is such instruction possible? I reply it is; it is necessary, and I would say to all Catholics, all Christians really anxious for their faith, If you wish to produce souls religiously convinced, renounce all false systems of a "Science without God," and introduce into the education and instruction of young men philosophy and religion—not the religion of the Catechism, but the religion of Theology. There are but two means of preserving their faith: either put them into a world apart, send them into deserts or mountains in order that they shall not breathe the air tainted with false doctrines—in short, prevent their thinking or living; or make of them serious intelligences and learned believers—if you like, theologians. This is, I know, only possible with exceptional minds; but the others have nothing to fear. A limited intelligence is in no danger from bad Science, since it is not open to good. Have no fear for it; God protects such by their very simplicity. Build, if you will, hospitals for the sick; but make camps for the valiant and the robust. To seek for the dying is a good work; to strengthen the living is a better.

That about which I am before all anxious, is the open intelligence; that which touches my heart is the young man whom I see grow up with eyes full of intelligence, a countenance full of candour, a soul full of passion. This it is that absorbs my interest; this it is that I seek to reach. I do not want to save the sick; it is the living that I would cure. Well, then, I tell this young man, "If you would keep inviolate your faith, you must study. If you would defend yourself against the unbeliever, you must know more than he."

To teach one's self is not easy; to understand one's religion in spirit and in truth is no slight task. Where shall we go? After twenty years of age there is no more school for a young man; and yet it is then that one must learn. It is not at fifteen that one can measure the life of Christ, and grasp the dimensions of that Divine Colossus who fills and rules all history, comprehend the immensity of the heavens to know what God has done, and see in the secular development of humanity the laws of Providence! You only take oath to defend the laws of your country at twenty; and it is as much as you can do at that age to comprehend the profundity of religion. You should study Science up to this age: but do not think that on leaving college you are a man; you know nothing yet, but that you may become one. Say to yourself only that the time has now come to study the great mysteries of the soul, to look into the unfathomable mysteries of God. Then perhaps you may be capable of reasoning upon high moral

L

truths, and of commencing at length the practical interpretation of the Catholic faith. For if there is a thing which demands in its study all earnestness of heart, all vigour of intelligence, all energy of youth, it is neither glory, nor ambition, nor love, nor Science; but it is the immortal destiny of the soul—it is Christ and God!

I also said that an armed and warlike instruction was necessary.

By these somewhat forcible expressions, which seem best to express my thought, I mean that there is a pacific instruction which prepares the soul simply to maintain its faith; and there is also a warlike and defensive instruction which prepares the soul to defend its faith, and which arms it against all objection.

Faith and religion are scientifically attacked; consequently a pacific instruction is no longer sufficient, and an aggressive instruction is imperative—I mean that instruction which concentrates the attention of the young man upon all those difficulties of which his faith can be the object, which does not content itself with setting forth the truth, but which will teach him the art of replying victoriously to the objection.

If we are not thus armed, brethren, if we do not see clearly all the manifold aggressions of which truth is the aim in literature, in history, in science, and in philosophy, we are vanquished. There will occur a phenomenon, very common to-day, and which, to my idea, is the most exact explanation of religious Scepticism in a great number of minds.

This phenomenon is a phenomenon of oscillation. They do not deny; they do not believe; they hesitate. They say, "*If*, however, this is not true? *If* Christ is no more than a man? If God is but the emanant law of things? If the future life is but a dream? Without doubt, I believe; but—but——" There are *buts* in the faith of believers; and every sincere mind not willing to live in an illusion discovers these *buts*. But, you may have asked yourselves, to what does this lead? It leads to the many objections which have not been answered in a precise, evident, and unflinching manner. Every objection unanswered carries into the soul the sting of doubt; it is a ball that has struck us, and has not been extracted. It travels in our body, and we cannot move without exclaiming, "It is there; I feel it!" Well, then, it is time that the objections should be vanquished and the ball extracted.

Let us be careful not to say to the man who doubts, "Silence the difficulty, drive it out." No; we must say to him, "Triumph over the difficulty; it is a necessary work, and the solidity and honour of your convictions depend on it."

Beside the pastor who keeps the faithful, beside the apostle announcing to those who have never heard it the good tidings of the Gospel, beside the traditional doctor teaching what has always been taught, I call, then, the doctor armed and militant, who can grasp every difficulty and give the reply without hesitation, who does not wait for the attack, but carries the battle into the enemy's ranks, and bravely takes the offensive. We have pastors that the whole world admires; we have apostles fearless in carrying their message of peace and consolation; we have even doctors buried in old parchments, initiated in all ancient tradition; we require younger doctors, who live in the enemy's camp and surprise the objection even before it is raised—a valiant legion, holding the sword of the Spirit, marching before to clear aside the doctrines of death, and show the road to those intelligences which to-day can see it no longer.

Let this legion haste, for night draws nigh. Why, O men of God, are you not there to translate into modern language those ancient truths, the eternal patrimony of believing souls? You announce to us the mysteries of God, but your words do not reach us. Speak to us, then, in a language we can understand. We have lost all memory of our childhood's tongue—it is possible, O doctors! Speak to us, then, in our barbaric dialect. What matter the expression? It is the truth we want; it is the truth whose privation is killing us.

Pray, my brethren, that the great Gospel may shine forth, and with it faith revive! It will revive only when we come in a mass to announce to this world, which no longer understands them, the mysteries of God. It wants the teaching, we well know, we who are of this age, who share the blood of this same youth, its aspirations, its hopes; we who know its intelligence and the objections which torture it. The day on which we come to interpret God it will understand and hold us out its hand. If to-day it turns from us, be assured it is only that we debase before it Him whom we can never exalt.

It is wrong that it should be so, say those without pity. Doubtless, the world is wrong to be sick at heart, to be weak, to have a bullet in the head; but, nevertheless, it is both sick and wounded. Take your part, then, and drive away the clouds from these lost and wounded creatures; blow upon this thick mist, and make a new star shine before them.

Who would let these perish? They can live only by the truth, but it must be the entire truth. The earthly light of Science will not suffice; being exclusive, it blinds instead of enlightening. The undecided teaching of a mutilated philosophy is not enough for the greatness of the problems that must be solved. They require the oracles of Eternity. Be it our task, then, to translate them.

FIFTH DISCOURSE.

PRACTICAL ATHEISM.

My Brethren,
The word of command is given: the mind of man is to be imprisoned in the universe and divorced from God.

All these systems tend to this divorce and limit us: positivism by suppressing the principle of causality, and closing every road by which reason raises itself to God; materialism by applying the same principle of causality, and binding us down to that matter which it makes the universal cause; atheistic pantheism by confessing a false Infinite, identical with the world, emanant but not transcendent cause of all things.

Beware of these systems, my brethren. If you accept them, you are enclosed in the universe without power to leave it. Call it, if you like, a collection of phenomena with positivism, an atom of matter with materialism, the great All with pantheism—it matters little what name—and the universe will be the gaol and your spirit the prisoner; and we can say of the prison with the poet—

"Over the door they wrote. God is forbidden to enter."

Is this work of Atheism possible? Why not? People say there is no such thing as an Atheist; there cannot be. Those who proclaim themselves as such deceive themselves; their heart protests against their thought, and their inward thought gives the lie to the words which fall from their lips. Doubtless man is not born Atheist, but he can become so; and what is necessary? To drive away God from your soul; to say to Him, "Away! you importune me." To say to that thought which is called the idea of God, "Away from me, phantom!" To say to the love of the Infinite, "You are my torture, I will stifle you!" To say to that Supreme Law which is called God, "Heavy chain, it is time that I should break you!" To cry, indeed, before those perspectives of eternity of which no intelligent being will ever fathom the depths, "Let a curtain fall for ever and hide from my sight this horizon which is my torment. There arise from thence spectres which I would fain dismiss."

Strange and revolting language! Well, man is capable of speaking thus. A free being, he can banish from his heart a friend, from his thoughts an image which oppresses him; he can also expel God.

Then he enters upon Practical Atheism. He soon lives as though God did not exist. He never thinks of God, or only at rare intervals. He does not like Him; God is indifferent to him. He does not fear, he forgets Him. He does not invoke Him; he treats Him as a stranger. Unbridled passions drift him along; he plunges madly into the wave, and cannot master it in God's name. In the day of anguish, when every creature lifts up its head and cries aloud to God, he remains stolid, without a prayer, without blasphemy, and his sorrow weighs upon him like the marble of a tomb. How many men there are to-day given over to this Atheism! How many sorrowful women driven into these desolate regions! Before plunging into the abyss, the heart of a woman is more than once troubled; her religious soul recoils and hesitates. Man is precipitated into it with violence. He also endeavours to stay himself upon the fatal incline to which the whirlwind of business, of passion, and of doctrine drags him, but in vain; the whirlwind carries him away, and the man succeeds but too well in driving God from his home, his hearth, and his country. Nations, in turn, banish God from their laws; they live as though Providence had never watched over their race, blessed their standards, conducted their armies to victory, sanctioned their laws, presided over their destinies.

But, meanwhile, think not that, having arrived at this state, men can live in tranquillity. Atheism is not a habitable land; it is a breakwater in a stormy sea, a bleak rock, against which you may be thrown and mangled, but on which you cannot land.

Do I need the aid of metaphysics, of speculative and abstract reason, to prove to the Atheist how weak and ineffectual his efforts against God are— to show him how tragic is his despairing doctrine? No; I will bring it home to him by that which touches his very heart and soul, the strongest and most living witness of God in the world.

Two things prevent him, then, from tranquil enjoyment of the sloth and oblivion he desires, and rise up like nightmares to startle him out of his lethargy.

The first is injustice victorious.

My brethren, you have all, have you not, met with crime triumphant? You have seen men and nations tortured by injustice and crushed by tyranny? Before such a spectacle, have you said with a bitter resignation, "It is a stroke of fate"? What conclusion would you draw? The conclusion *I* draw is—God. How! an innocent being is persecuted by the world, an honest man succumbs and dies, branded by injustice, and you say, "So much the worse for him!" Well, I do *not* say "so much the worse," my brethren. Conscience, too, does not say "so much the worse." No; she rises up from the block upon which the head has fallen, she mounts the scaffold upon which the blood of the just has been outpoured, as if it were an altar, and looking higher than the earth, she cries, "I appeal to God, who sees and judges. To-day is the hour of injustice; to-morrow it will be that of justice and retribution. I can wait."

My brethren, one may be an Atheist during the

intoxication of pleasure; earthly joys frequently hide heaven from our eyes. One is never an Atheist when struggling against injustice. There have been scientific Atheists, Atheistic writers and false poets, and Atheistic politicians; but do you know where Practical Atheism has never yet been found? Amongst those who were persecuted for righteousness' sake—amongst the martyrs. The executioners indeed may be Atheists; the victims never.

O outraged, oppressed conscience! Thou art the last inviolable refuge whither, to defy those who would banish Him, God withdraws Himself. There, brethren, He is invincible.

To be a martyr is not given to all. Some live their life here without ever encountering injustice; they die innocent and blest without having had to tremble before the executioner, and quit this world serene and happy, as though no evil existed and wrong never triumphed over right. Such are the elect and chosen of God, blessed by His peculiar providence and raised above this world of strife.

But, my brethren, there is one thing we have all known. Does the man live whose heart has not been touched at least once? Does the man live who has not felt his heart beat more rapidly, and who has not at some time said, "I love. I love that one who is good, honest, and noble; whose affection has given me life, whose soul vibrates in unison with mine"? Nevertheless, however vehement the love, a fatal hour arrives, the beloved soul passes away, and that soul into whose very depths we have looked, and where we had fixed our every hope and longing, that second self leaves us!

Then, brethren, when we love, and when we behold the death of those we love, I ask, is Atheism possible?

Before the open gulf of the tomb, what says positivism to the anguished heart? It is silent. But it is just that which makes us despair. Pushed to extremity, it talks vaguely of the survival of humanity. Humanity? What does that mean? And again the lost one even there remains but a recollection—but it is not a recollection I want, it is a living reality—*that* alone will suffice me! Ah! you who no longer believe in God, be silent before love made desperate by death; utter silence is better than illusory consolation.

And the materialist? What can he offer to the despairing heart? Nothing; only his eternal "matter." He may turn and twist it as he likes, but he cannot find in it consolation for the smallest grief, nor the power to dry a single tear. The pantheist in his turn invokes in anguish his shadowy "Infinite;" but this blind and inexorable force, which produces everything without thought, and destroys them impassibly, can but add to our despair.

You then who have loved, and whose heart cries out full of hope, "I can carry my love with me into eternity!" if you are without God, bury your love together with the beloved one in the grave: all is finished. There is no other alternative; you must choose between faith and despair.

God suppressed, the supremely good and intelligent One thrust away, our horizon darkens; it becomes veiled in impenetrable clouds, and all those who cease to believe in God knock in vain at the door of the tomb to discover its secret. Despair is the only reply.

O sceptic! O Atheist! I leave you to your doctrines and your despair! There is no need for argument here. Keep them, keep the mournful light of your heartless Science! *I* will confess before all Him to whom I owe the love which gives life to my soul, and who alone assures me of its immortality. Against that death which would crush me God is my only refuge; and in the name of Christ I defy it.

Before the presence of Right struggling with Might, before Love struggling against Death, be not surprised, my brethren, that the believer should rise up with supreme energy, and that his faith should become invincible. In what is it astonishing that the vibration of our heart should give forth a sound incomprehensible to Science? Must one renounce necessary truth because our hearts and consciences proclaim them more strongly perhaps than our reason?

I have already spoke to you of the great German philosopher Kant; I mention him again, as he has in this age and country considerable influence over men's minds. Kant has written two books, "The Criticism of Pure Reason" and "The Criticism of Practical Reason." You think, possibly, that both these books lead to the same conclusion ? Not at all. In the first, with regard to the logical and ontological principles of things, Kant is a sceptic. He says, "The human mind has its form; it sees realities as *it* is, not as they are," and Kant cannot conclude the objective reality of the conceptions of reason. But, in the "Criticism of Practical Reason," his destructive analysis is arrested. What has it encountered? That which we call love and justice; Kant calls it duty, a more vigorous term for a philosopher. The patriarch of sceptics, wiser and more intelligent than the philosophers of to-day, before duty retraces his steps. "Duty is a reality!" he exclaims. "In the presence of duty I bow down." He believes in the objective reality of the truths of practical reason, he upsets the doctrine of his previous work, and, not afraid to contradict himself, constructs upon duty a complete theodicy.

Brethren, this example, borrowed from the land of doubt, is neither catholic nor Christian. No matter; I quote it on the side of reason, as against those who shelter themselves under the genius of Kant, in order to destroy reason: they should at least, like him, respect the impassable limits before which even his daring criticism was arrested. But no, these limits are violated perpetually. Atheism increases and takes possession of souls. Those young men to whom I speak will bear me out in this. Those who, being young, are sincere and open, and who do not fear to say what passes in their minds, and whose minds feel most keenly and impetuously the struggle of doubt and belief—those, I say, will not hesitate, if I ask them, to admit it. "Yes, we are carried away from God. What demon drags us we know not; but faith and old beliefs are without attraction for us, we are fascinated by those doctrines which assail them so furiously. Enthusiasm for the things of heaven is extinct; we have scarcely any for the things of the earth. Our blood is frozen. It seems as though a long day was just ended, and that an immense chilly night was gradually falling around us."

Behold the doctrines which are leading this generation astray! These are the systems advocated in successful books, taught by renowned professors. Public favour is on their side; the people applaud without understanding them; men of letters cringe —often without replying. Take care, my brethren! Beware the consequences of error; they are terrible, like those brain maladies which betray no sign of their existence, and which, long hidden, break forth in some sudden and tragical death! People are only anxious about the visible and the immediate; they are reassured by false appearances. They say, "There will always be time to think about that to-morrow." What indeed do you see, you careful ones? You see very far when your possessions are menaced. Statesmen, what do you see? You see very clearly when your power is in danger. Ministers and leaders of your country, what do you see? You see the danger when the frontier of a country is threatened. But that the doctrine of a whole race or nation should be attainted, that the brain of a whole generation should be deformed, by an unhealthy education and dissolute teaching, who cares? who is anxious? You cry out when incendiaries burn your houses, when a rebellious mob overturns a throne, or when the stranger invades your land; but do you ask what incites the incendiary, what ideas undermine your power, what crimes draw down upon your country defeat and invasion? You ask yourselves so little these questions, that in the presence of the very doctrines which produce these scourges you are silent; and when a book has appeared and eloquent voices have spoken, or the blood of some great criminal has flowed, you go to sleep again, satisfied that truth and justice are sufficiently avenged. What is the good? there are other things quite as important. Nothing, brethren—not even your financial security, not even your social security, not even your political security—nothing, I tell you, is more important than the truth; for financial, social, and political security have but one single corner-stone: truth. It is by truth that everything resists and triumphs; it is by error that everything falls to pieces and perishes. And if you do not watch over the truth which is assailed on all sides, your decadence is prepared; you are marked for death.

Ah! if I could but instil into the souls of this generation, of this whole country, my convictions and my ardour, my fears and my hopes, there would rise up among us men of prudence and daring, as resolute in defending the truth as others in defending property. Property is the truth embodied in a little land; truth is property in the divine estate, that of conviction. Property does not exist by itself; it has a foundation—right. And what is right, but truth?

Thus, brethren, you see yourselves obliged to watch, under pain of death, over that truth of which Atheism is the ruin. Let us come, then, to fact, and expose the consequences of a life without God. In the question of Practical Atheism society and the soul are directly interested; the soul as the focus of all human activity, society as the sphere in which that activity moves.

What effect has the suppression of God on the soul?

First of all, what is the soul? Four words reveal it: truth, rectitude, love, and happiness. Truth; for the soul is intelligent and seeks only to know it. Rectitude: the soul is free and honest, and must respect it. Love: the soul was not created alone, it is from the beginning family and nation; it is created to love. Happiness: it is the cry of all, that is, of all that lives; it is the insatiable passion of the intelligent free and living soul. Thus you have in four words the secret of yourselves, a secret long sought for, perhaps, and hiding many joys and many sorrows, much greatness and much misery.

Put into a being thus formed Practical Atheism, what becomes of the truth? It becomes simply a torment, because it is made an impossibility. If we suppress God we can never arrive at that truth we long to know, and from henceforth our intelligence is condemned to a long martyrdom. What indeed do you as intelligent beings wish most of all to know? The nature and property of things? The little mysteries of the earth, or the great mysteries of heaven? No, nothing of all that Science can show us, when we have fathomed its first elements and its supreme conclusions can satisfy us. Science? It treats only of phenomena, our intelligence seeks to know that which is beneath; it does not stop at the consequence, it wishes to know the cause. Now, brethren, Atheism suppresses the principle and the cause, and if it consents to leave them to us, it puts before us a false principle and a ridiculous cause, which not only does not explain things, but does not even explain itself. But what do I say? It stops us brusquely, in the name of positivism. According to it, we must no longer seek for a principle or a cause; we are limited absolutely to phenomena. But we repudiate the declarations of positivism—humanity has never submitted to them; and it is not after the long experience of centuries that we are to be persuaded that they will accept them to-day. The surface of our nature may vary, its essential wants are unalterable. We have always sought for God, we always seek for Him obstinately and restlessly, and we find Him as far as He can be known and found by our darkened intelligence. We seek for Him and find Him, not experimentally, but with metaphysical reason and those principles of eternal truth which allow us to grasp the cause from the

M

effect, the substance from the phenomenon, under the veil of creation to discover the infinite God.

Doubtless, left to ourselves, we could not penetrate by our own strength the Universal Cause, nor see with our eyes the Absolute Principle; but the little that our weak reason can discover already responds to the deep aspirations of our soul.

We cannot see that inapproachable Being, but we know that He is. The road which leads to Him is open to us; our intelligence leads us thither step by step; as it advances the prospect becomes wider, and light is added to light. Even if we were to be ever struggling towards God without ever reaching Him, even if the Catholic faith did not assure us of His ineffable possession, we ought not to complain of the lot to which our finite nature condemns us. The torture does not consist in pursuing a path full of light; it consists in feeling that that path is closed against us. Now, Atheism in every form inflicts this torture upon us; and it endeavours by every means to construct in our minds an impenetrable barrier, which shall shut out the heavens, in which we behold afar off the inaccessible form of God.

Practical men will perhaps say, "Speculative truth does not matter to us; the mere object of mental contemplation, it has no direct action upon practical life." What, then, let me ask, guides men? What should order their conduct and direct all their actions? Right and moral law. Now, without God, what becomes of righteousness as an absolute law? I should much like to be told.

Right, you will tell me, is that which has been accepted by the multitude. By the multitude? Then the majority is always right? Right means a hundred thousand men! And if these hundred thousand men crush me—if they crucify me? What, it was the Romans, the executioners of Christ, who were doing right? In the name of which right did they crucify Him? For Pilate pretended to have the right on his side, and the Jews on theirs. Right, then, is something quite relative; it is that which those who deny God, and no longer see in that moral law which explains the absolute connection of things a reflex of the Infinite, are obliged to admit. My brethren, right is either absolute or it is not. It is necessary or it is not. It is neither number nor force that determines it; it is not even originated by reason. Reason does not create it—she proves it; she is not the author, but the witness. No, indeed! Force in this matter would be worse even than the multitude. Right is not originated—it exists. But where? What intelligence would be found its immutable domain when you have suppressed God?

Nothing remains but humanity, which is might and majority? Once more, this cannot be.

When conscience—that is, right—is on your side, you stand firm in your superiority, armed with moral force, and raised on the pedestal of justice; and in the name of God, who consecrates right, you say, "Stand back!" to the mob; and to brute force you cry, "There is the barrier; there is my right. You take it from me; I protest. And before God I remain the sole true master."

Though centuries should pass, though millions of worlds should have made their evolutions, right remains ever the same; and its truth, whatever savants say, will stand for ages, like the granite rocks, when the power of the multitude has wasted itself and vanished away like the angry foam of the sea. The right has been ever the same, from the beginning of the world till now; always Christ's law of love, uprightness, and self-sacrifice; and though at first seen dimly, its outlines have never changed, only Christianity revealed its utmost perfection of detail.

That which I have said concerning right we can also say of love. The soul is formed to lean towards those sympathetic beings whom Providence has chosen and reserved for it: towards the father and mother; towards that first group called the family; towards that chosen group called friends; towards that more extended group called a nation, a race; towards that yet vaster group called humanity. We are not alone; the solitary man is an incomprehensible and repulsive being. Our natural want is to love outside ourselves.

Well! believe me, if you suppress God by Practical Atheism, you wound love mortally; you stifle it by limiting its duration and its intensity, and you no longer leave it a guarantee against death. Without God no soul is immortal. Now, affection is like right; it is eternal and without limit, or it is not. If you end, if you are but the being of a day, what is the good of loving? Happy to-day, to-morrow you weep in anguish over a black, hopeless grave, which swallows up your all, and leaves you nothing—the tomb without resurrection! If I were to advise this ephemeral being, I should say to him, " Go into the desert, and alone, before the immensity which surrounds you, gaze upon the dust from which you were made, that which has had the insolence to place you here; look, and curse everything, but love nothing."

Is this a Satanic counsel? No, indeed, it is that of a friend. Things must, of course, be judged by their utility. Why deceive yourself? it is neither good nor wise. Would you think a man sensible who went voluntarily to the galleys, to endure the suffering of a convict? All those who do not believe in God and an immortal soul, and yet allow themselves to love intensely, voluntarily chain themselves to a weight, and consent to drag it about with them. If you no longer believe in God or in the soul, if you are an Atheist, I see nothing better for you than to harden your heart till it is a stone, if you can; it may be brutal, but it is at least intelligent and dignified: but wilfully to love under such conditions is insane.

How, after that, can we speak of happiness? What! when you can never attain the truth which is your natural longing, or obtain that right which is the rule and the honour of your conduct, or enjoy that love which is the perfume of life, you speak of happiness? What a mockery in the very word! I understand bliss for those living in the light, knowing no limit to their visions of divine goodness, seeing right respected around them, and able to labour at making it respected, crowned by justice, and able to exclaim, "My life expands in the ecstasy of a deep love blessed and sanctified by God; it will know no decline; it will be more blessed than the suns by which it is measured; for they pass away, but my love is immortal." But with Practical Atheism we bid adieu to these sacred things, and thus, also, to our happiness; for what is our happiness made up of, if not of truth, of justice, and of love?

Go, then, you who believe no more in happiness and are unable any longer to believe in it! Pursue your road without any end but despair and its dark gulf. Go! *I* will not follow you. Will you, my brethren? Will *you* descend into this hell? There was written above the gates of that hell seen by the poet in his sublime and fantastic vision—

"All Hope abandon, ye who enter here!"

My brethren, Dante's hell might be a paradise compared with the darkness into which Practical Atheism plunges the human soul. On the threshold of this black gulf do you know what is written? "All truth, all right, all love, abandon, ye who enter here!" If it was merely leaving your happiness, who would not enter heroically into the gulf and leave it behind them like a cast-off rag? But no: it is truth that we must abandon; it is right that must be trodden underfoot; it is love that must be outraged and martyred! You are not capable of this! If I would drag you thither, your conscience would rise up like an armed man, and cry, "Away from me!" My brethren, it is not to me that you must say this; it is to those systems I have denounced. Cry it aloud, then, and with all the eloquence of your soul!

We are not only individuals, we are members of a nation and a race. For that reason Atheism has first to be considered with regard to individual existence, and afterwards with regard to social life. Now, the whole problem of social life may be summed up thus: it is necessary that those who govern should not oppress, otherwise we are no longer subjects, but slaves; it is necessary that those who are governed should be united, should help each other, and should not revolt against those who govern, otherwise we are no longer free citizens, but rebels.

These are the Scylla and Charybdis of all nations: oppression from those who govern, rebellion amongst those who are governed—to express the thing in two words, antagonism of the social elements. Where this antagonism is, that nation's decay is certain, its dissolution imminent. You may call it a nation, it is one only in name. It is said to be alive, it is dead; it is a corpse, whose wrappings and perfumes disguise neither its stench nor its decomposition.

Well, when Atheism is established in a nation, that nation—I do not know in how long a time; but what matter the time if the event is fatal?—to a certainty comes to oppression on the part of those who govern, and rebellion in those who are governed. Yes, oppression from above, rebellion from below; this is the climax. I will prove it.

What are the guarantees of the governed against the governing? These latter are the masters; they have intelligence, the administration, the police, the army, the revenues; they hold in their hands all the public force. Against them, I repeat, what is our protection? Can you tell me? Besides, there are things that are beyond the power of protection; our goods, our children, our family, our lives, how do I know? The all-powerful State may say, "I want your fortune; I have millions to pay. I want your children; war is declared. I want your life; it is necessary for my security." What could you answer to these despotic exactions of an unbridled Government?

In all history there is but one power which has victoriously held its own against political government and the abuse of power by brute force. You do not perhaps know this power? Yes, you know it well; it is conscience. This it is which you must at all cost keep inviolate, defend from tyranny, and surround with an absolute respect. If all is oppressed, violated, enslaved, let conscience remain safe, free, and untainted. Until Christ it was in the hands of Cæsars and emperors, and the State which passed religious as well as political laws, as it dictated them to all else, so it imposed them upon the conscience. It said, "I want not only your fortune—your fortune is mine; not only your slave—your slave is mine; not only your life—your life is mine! Everything belongs to me, even your conscience."

Now, brethren, there arose in the midst of centuries a Man whom France to-day blasphemes, whom writers dare to insult in the name of a Science that they make to lie, a Man whose divine aureole they take away, a Man—should I say "man" in speaking of Him that is God?—this Man has taken the conscience, and has said to it, "Come unto Me, I will be your freedom. I am no master, but the God that created you." He has cried to the Cæsars of every name, age, and country, "Away with you, oppressors! I leave you the kingdoms of this world. Fortune tempts you; take it! You want young men for your wars; take them! You want human hecatombs; let blood flow round your homicidal thrones! One day you will see these floods staunched, but henceforth there is something which belongs to Me, which is of the least of these little ones, something you shall not touch!" "What?" they ask in surprise. They *have* asked it. Well, Christ has answered, "That something is conscience!" They have accused the successors of Christ, the great Liberator, of having used oppression; it is not for me to excuse nor to vindicate them. Did not Christ say, "Go, take under your religious sway, under your invisible sceptre, the conscience of man, not to subjugate it, but to snatch it from the power of the sword, from the tyranny of the mighty in this world. You are simple, ignorant, unarmed; go, in spite of all: whatever you do in this world to free the soul and the conscience will be approved in heaven." By virtue of this word, humanity, which before knew only masters, has known liberators. But remember, brethren, that the great fellow-workers with Christ in liberating the conscience believed in God, and that they adored Him Incarnate.

Well, the day on which you extirpate God from your race and country, you will renew the confusion of temporal and spiritual power, the subjection of the priesthood to the empire, of the cross to the sword; and the God you have driven from heaven you will find on a throne avenging and implacable, changed to a Moloch, weighing down your conscience even under the very yoke you thought you had thrown off. You may have suppressed the Pope perhaps; but with the Pope you will have suppressed also liberty of conscience.

It is not worth while to call yourselves free beings, and boast of your Science and your new world, since by banishing God you have chained up the highest faculties of your intelligence, and stamped out the most sacred feelings of humanity.

If you allow Atheism to invade the people, you will see develop, with oppression in high places, revolution in the low; you will see arise, spread, increase beyond measure that which is called so aptly in the language of to-day, "The popular wave." It will rise like a resistless sea. Perhaps it will come slowly; you take it for a calm, ordinary tide, and think you can predict exactly how high it will rise, and when its swollen waves will subside. The sea creeps up formidable, all-powerful; an invisible force urges it to rise. What is this force? Envy, jealousy, hatred, all the angry passions which the sight of social inequality arouses in souls hungry for enjoyment; these differences of wealth and position are so painful, so bitter to those who have lost faith in Providence, and with it the divine secret of suffering and resignation. Can you, then, show me the way to master these passions, which lie smouldering within a nation like the fire within a volcano? You count, I know, upon brute force. You think to say to this people, "If you revolt, I have soldiers and guns; I have prisons and police." Under these threats a people may be calmed, but not for long. There is something stronger than servile fear, stronger than the tyrant—the unchained human soul. There comes a time—we have seen it, and the former generation has seen it—a moment of terrible exasperation, which nothing can restrain, which breaks down the barriers that you thought so strong, and the wave rises irresistibly.

Ah! if to all the discontented, to all those weary of life, to all who suffer, who are hungry and athirst, you would but teach charity; if you sent them apostles to say to them, as Saint Paul did to the slaves, "You are sons of the same Father who is in heaven!" if, leading their souls to God, you would teach them that above every creature there is the Infinite, and that beyond this world there is eternity—you would save them and you would save yourselves; there would henceforth be a hope for these souls that wander hopelessly upon the earth, and a cure for those passions which become excited by hate into a frenzy. Far from doing this, we are striving to eradicate God from the souls of the people. We close our eyes to the consequences of such a work, and we tranquilize our minds by saying, "Men are good, why should we doubt them? Men are weak, we know how to restrain them." Well, my brethren, be warned; know that under many and changing appearances the soul is ever the same, a passionate being not to be exasperated with impunity, whose explosions may prove fatal. The ocean does not change either: it breaks against its dykes to-day as it did yesterday; it rises and falls; it has the same fury and the same tempests.

The people are like the grey sea that the active and intrepid people of Holland have banked out with dykes constructed by their own hands. One day an insect, brought over in the planks of a ship from some distant continent, got into the wood of these dykes. The Dutch work; they are proud of the land they have conquered from the ocean; it is green and prosperous; all the wealth of nations comes into their ships, and adds to the prosperity of this enterprising and industrious little kingdom. All at once there was a hole in the dyke; the invisible insect had eaten through the barrier raised up against the sea, to the very last grain. The people in distress rushed from their houses and their shops; there was but one cry raised—" To the dykes ! "

Brethren, the sea of Holland is popular passion, passion amongst the high and amongst the low, a veritable ocean which may to-morrow break into this country and submerge it. The insect which gnaws the dyke silently and fatally, that insect is the teaching of a " Science without God ! " Brethren, beware ! Fathers and mothers, sons and young girls, all of you, be up and doing. " To the dykes ! " To-morrow, perhaps, it may be too late.

SIXTH DISCOURSE.

THE EXISTENCE OF GOD.

BRETHREN,

Does God exist? Positivism replies, "This is a useless and unintelligible question; we have suppressed Him." Materialism replies, "Matter and its forces alone exist, and matter is God." Pantheism replies, "The great All alone exists, and the great All is God." Scepticism replies, "I don't know."

And we, my brethren, what shall we say?

Amongst those who proclaim the existence of God, some regard it as a first truth which needs no demonstration. At the first glance it is grasped by their intelligence. God is; for those understanding the value of terms, that is equivalent to this: Being is. Thus there is no proposition of more sure and irresistible evidence possible.

Others say, "Do not attempt to prove the existence of God; it is above the power of any human intelligence. Faith may proclaim God, reason can only suspect His existence. Faith affirms, reason doubts." Has not Pascal written, in one of his impetuous moments, "We are incapable of knowing what God is, or if He exists." And traditionalists who have wished to build up revelation on the ruins of human intelligence, the necessary basis of all faith, have repeated Pascal's words and stupidly professed scepticism.

Thus the existence of God is to some a self-evident truth; to others a truth beyond human intelligence. In both cases its demonstration is useless; it is either supererogatory or powerless.

We do not accept these extreme doctrines.

If the existence of God is a self-evident truth, why do so many men dare to doubt it? They deny it, I know, only with their lips and in their heart, but is it natural for heart and lips to deny first truths? Those who do so it is impossible to argue with; it is only possible to leave them to their folly—all evidence and demonstration is wasted on such persons. But atheism is not of this kind; the very highest intellects have used their best powers in endeavouring to rise to this truth, which is proclaimed by all around us to those who are capable of hearing its voice.

To those who believe that the existence of God cannot be established by reason, permit me to reply with some energy. How! born of God, created for him, has man neither in his heart, his intelligence, nor his soul, the means of finding his Father and calling upon Him? How! He that has created us intelligent and given us hearts to love Him, shall He have refused us the power of knowing Him? This is repugnant to common sense.

For our parts, brethren, we do not believe in God; we prove Him.

The existence of God is a demonstrable truth, and it must be demonstrated, as the denial of it is everywhere insolently proclaimed, and is asserted under forms even more lying than audacious.

My brothers, there are three books in which to-day every one reads: the book of Nature, the book of the soul, and the book of history. Nature bears engraved in letters of splendour the name of God; it furnishes that argument which we may call experimental. The soul bears this name in letters of fire, and furnishes that argument which we call psychological. History writes it in letters of brilliancy and majesty; it gives us that argument which we call historical. Now, if nature proclaims with its grand voice, and the soul cries out in unison, that there is a God, and if history joins nature and the soul in this solemn attestation, who shall dare to mutiny against this sacred and threefold testimony?

Yes, God exists, and Nature demonstrates Him. Whosoever interrogates her with common sense, with poetry, with the most advanced Science, will find her proclaim to every unprejudiced mind and sincere heart that God exists, and that He is the principle, the law, and the end. Nature is that exterior life which man perceives around him, which he observes and tests by his experience. Now, brethren, when Science wishes to show us Nature, what does she do? She studies the living things around us; traces out their birth, their development, and their death; she compares them, defines the characteristics which assimilate or distinguish them, and by the extent of her investigations is enabled to grasp and to explain the very essence of things, as well as their *ensemble*.

This *ensemble* in its totality cannot be perceived by human eyes. We see a speck in the universe, but not the entire universe. Assisted by wonderful instruments, we see very far into space; but the farther we see, the more the horizon opens, the wider the perspective appears; the more worlds we discover the more there are to be discovered—the unknown multiplies itself at each step of Science. The progress of Science is mathematical, the progress of the unknown is geometrical. And so, in advancing into the territory of the unknown, Science has her hours of lassitude, and we hear her, the light, the indefatigable seeker, confess hopelessly her obscurity and her impotence.

But what does she prove in that domain open to her search? What does she discover in beings with life and without, in those that can be put under a microscope and those that can only be reached by the most powerful telescope? What is the great phenomenon of organic and inorganic life, of the infinite detail as of the incommensurable whole? In a word, what is this Nature? Science interrogates it every day; what name has she discovered for it?

Well, its chiefest characteristic, its very essence, the name found for it by that Science which is ever studying and analyzing it, is motion: that which changes progresses and is transformed. Perpetual motion, activity always and everywhere, quiescence never and in no place. Quiescence is an illusion. Where we see only inertia, invisible forces work and move; they balance but do not destroy each other. Repose is movement in equilibrium.

Again, in its *ensemble*, as in its detail, to the eye of advanced Science Nature is not only a moving but a *progressive* force. Nature is not; she grows. It is she that should be called the perpetual " to be," not God. We only see her partially: her immensity escapes us; we perceive only our globe, its satellites, and our solar system. We can only give a glance at the nebulæ in the midst of which we are lost; we catch sight of, but cannot fathom, that wonderful Milky Way in which we float like a leaf lost in the ocean. But in that particle of Nature which has been explored by Science, what is the prominent feature? An orderly, incessant, progressive activity, destroying at times, but to build up anew. Whence goes this progress? To what goal is it pushing? Is it difficult to discover? Matter progresses towards life; its tendency is to condense itself for the formation of habitable globes. Science beholds this miracle. Although not born when it was accomplished, she is able to evoke it; she goes back into the immensity of ages; she says to all this past, to all these dead, "Shake off the dust of your tombs; it is I that summon you!"

Centuries have come forth from the darkness; the dead have declared their names; fossils have reappeared; whole creations have answered, "Behold us!" and recounted their past history and the miracle of their appearance in an inert world, incapable of producing them, yet seeming to wait for their arrival.

See you the work of Science? She wishes to examine and unravel this Nature. See how she makes it obey her. Science follows the progress of the cosmos step by step. She sees matter condense itself into immense bodies to serve as an abode for life. At first all is rough, silent, chaotic. Then order begins; geometry traces its lines, its circumferences, its ellipses. Every body and every mass follows the pre-ordained line, circumference, and ellipse; and all this is performed by those minute invisible atoms which we cannot grasp, but can only divine, and which, like the great celestial bodies, have their geometry and follow their pre-arranged route. The work is of absolute regularity; all combines to raise a pedestal for something greater than itself, an abode for some one more worthy.

When the abode is prepared the guest arrives; when the pedestal is raised the statue is placed upon it. The pedestal is the inorganic, the statue the organic world; the abode is the geometric world, built like a temple whose every angle is measured with the wisest harmony. Nature makes a step; it rises to the living being: this is the pre-destined guest.

It is born a mere nothing, a rudiment, without determinate form, which develops so far as to replenish in its fecundity the temple it inhabits. In the bosom of the protoplasm is formed a cellule, a species of utricle, in which is imprisoned a strange force which creates and destroys organic matter, which burns it, contracts and moves, living only on condition of dying, and, by multiplying itself, ends by absorbing all inert matter. This humble life in its apparent infirmity is master; the earth on which it is cast belongs to it—inert matter yields obedience to living matter. Atoms grow and combine in changeable proportions at the will of vital force. Life grows. It rises, becomes complex, and springs forth in that vegetable life whose fantastic marvels it is not for me to analyze, nor to describe the innumerable floræ that have succeeded each other on this planet or on other worlds.

Animal life appears. Nothing tires nature at work. Ever higher! it seems to say. The forms of the fauna develop little by little, the rudimentary types are refined and completed. But what matters this secondary work of elegance and refinement? The characteristic phenomenon of this new phase is the nervous system, that delicate and mysterious organization which is to serve as prelude, and also as foundation, to the being that feels, knows, and moves. Plants cannot move nor feel; animals do both, and the nervous system is their special attribute. And all the artifice of Nature, in the progressive elaboration to which it subjects matter, seems to tend to the production of this marvellous power, the last effort of organic life, the highest form of matter.

And whither go these multitudes of animals of

every form ranked in these grades into which Science endeavours to classify them? Have they no other destiny but to fill the world with their cries and their strifes? No! ever higher. The animal is but the sketch of a nobler and more perfect organization and life. After the inferior beings who know, feel, and move, behold the thinking being, free and able to command himself and to command all the rest. After the animal comes—man.

Not in vain was the earth formed, the clay fashioned, and the Divine breath breathed over all to animate and stir it; matter was to yield up all it contained, and after having served for sensation and instinct, it was still to be welded into the free and thinking being, and become the organic condition and support of intelligence and liberty. I have shown you, brethren, a page from the book of Nature. I have only interpreted into the language of modern Science what Moses wrote in the first chapter of the Bible.

To sum up, Nature is in motion. A progressive thing, she starts from the atom, and, going through the intermediate degrees to which I have directed your attention, she attains to thought. The atom is almost nothing; thought almost everything. Who takes into account an atom? Thought takes everything into account. The atom does not know itself; it does not know what surrounds it; it is solitary. Thought cannot ignore itself, nor be unconscious of what surrounds it. Thought is the reflector in which every being can leave its image; it is the wide glance over the universe of things.

Such, brethren, is the conclusion of experimental Science. She can only tell you this: In the beginning was the atom; in the end, thought; between, organization in every degree. Nothing more, nothing less. She will describe it some day, doubtless, with greater amplitude and perfection, but she will always stop where experience ends. This is so true, that those men who profess to recognize nothing but experimental Science advance as a principle that there is nothing more to look for. They are wrong. When experience ends, reason begins. The proof? Your own thoughts, whilst I am speaking to you. You are waiting; you seem to say to me, "When I know all that scientific observation can attain, shall I be any more advanced? The curiosity of my mind is but half satisfied. Phenomena succeed, but do not explain each other. Facts of history are the materials of Science; they are not the light." What seek you then? The cause and beginning of things. Without knowing it, almost in spite of yourself, you are in search of God.

Well, then, it is before the grand spectacle of the progress of the universe, that, armed by the principle of causality, eager to find the cause, our minds rise irresistibly towards God, sole and sovereign cause of the world studied by Science. This principle is merciless: there must be in the cause all that I see in the phenomenon, or the cause explains nothing, and does not give me the reason of phenomena. If a being moves, it must have a mover; it cannot move alone. The passivity of the being moved, and the activity of the mover, spring from the same origin. Now, when a being progresses from the imperfect to the perfect, from an inferior to a superior state, I must discover the cause of this superiority. It has it not in itself; for that would be a contradiction. In the same way, when a being progresses from a lifeless to a living state, I ask who has produced this progress? They tell me, lifeless matter. How! That which is without life can produce life! What a sophism! It would be denying the motive and first principle of reasoning, the principle of causality. Therefore there was in the commencement of things a Being, who by its own virtue contained all that we have seen unfolded through successive ages—a Being who is the reason of movement, of life, of sensation, and of thought.

I resume: Nature moves; therefore she has a first mover. Nature progresses; she goes from inert matter to the living state; therefore a living force must conduct her progress. Nature goes from inferior to more perfect life; therefore a living and perfect force must lead her. Nature, by man, who is highest in the scale of life on this planet, rises to thought; therefore a living, orderly, perfect, and intelligent force impels her. This living, orderly, perfect, intelligent force is God.

The catholic doctrine, my brethren, in accord with spiritual philosophy thus resolved the problem of the evolution of things: "In the beginning was the Word"—or Thought—" and the Word was with God, and the Word *was* God." Thought has produced the atom; thought has produced life; thought has produced that little flame, that ray that we call the soul of man. Thus Thought, or the Word, as Saint John says, was God. Therefore, brethren, the first Cause was God.

As in Nature a first Cause is necessary, so also is an aim. Progress cannot be aimless; it cannot lead to nothing. What, then, is this aim? It is perfection. All that is progresses from the imperfect to the perfect. If then in the narrow sphere of our experience we see all things progressing towards perfection, and serving each other as it were for a basis on which to rise towards a higher grade, we are forced to recognize as set before and in advance of all things, not annihilation, nor a vacuum, but the final Being—that One called by Aristotle the Desirable, because every creature desires Him, and towards Him all things move.

Thus, as we recognize in the beginning the activity which has produced all things, we also recognize, at the end and beyond, the Good, or that Perfection which attracts every being and determines its movement. From one point of view Nature becomes God. She seems in labour during ages without end, in space without limit, groaning to bring forth her infinite inaccessible perfection. God, the Beginning and End of things, is also the centre, or the Sovereign Law; for everything progresses according to a Law. Study Nature, you will see her ever following in the same paths, from which she never strays. Atoms ever follow the same direction, molecules are composed of the same atoms, all bodies obey an invariable impulse, living creatures retain ever the same form; if they depart from it, as in certain species, a power brings them back, sometimes roughly, to their type and starting-point. The forefather reappears. One directing idea pervades all things and fixes for everything that lives and is, its place and its trajectory. Nothing ever deviates from it; one only being has this melancholy privilege—man; but even when straying man renders homage to the supreme Law he infringes.

Thus does Nature, at least in its essential features, reveal its Author. At each page of the book God appears under the form of the Cause of movement, the End to which it is attracted, the Law which regulates it. The First Cause explains to us the starting-point of the divers grades in Nature; the End justifies that movement of impatience, innate in every being, which draws it towards perfection; the supreme Law, reuniting the Beginning and the End, accounts for the stability of the universe, and for the grandeur of the plan according to which all things are unfolded in time and space.

Such, brethren, is the divine testimony of the first book. Listen now to the evidence of the soul.

Nature is outside us; it is matter, a matter without a voice. The soul is the being which speaks, and as the doctors of the Church have called it, the being which is instructed of God: θεοδιδακτον.

It is impossible for any one who has looked, if only for a second, into that abyss which we call the soul, into that restless immensity called the human heart, where living forces are in a tumultuous activity of which the cosmic forces are but a faint image—it is impossible, I say, for any one who has done this, however slightly, to refuse to acknowledge the Infinite.

God has been pleased to set His mark in the soul of man. It is in the image of God; the rest has but a faint trace of Him. It is, then, in the soul that we must look to discover the Infinite. It is written in Genesis, "And they heard the voice of God walking in the garden in the cool of the day." The Eden, my brethren, is yourselves; the trees amongst which God walked, which gave Him a sacred shelter, are all that lives within you. And if you know how to listen, you will hear the footsteps of God therein, more clearly than in the earthly Eden.

My brethren, what is the human soul?

What are you? What am I—I who am speaking to you? What is that force which is above and outside Nature, which studies and divines it, which commands it with authority and transforms it at will? We are all conscious of it; the soul is a progressive, moving, struggling force. But whither does it go? towards what is it in progress? All advances, and is in evolution in Nature. If the soul is but a force in evolution, then it becomes confounded with Nature. Not so; the soul has a character which distinguishes it from everything outside it. Things move and stop. Atoms move and stop. Living cellules move and stop. All they can do is to raise themselves to become an agent of thought, a particle of that nervous substance which forms the pinnacle of the pyramid of matter.

When, after a thousand combinations and metamorphoses, the atom has reached this point, what becomes of it? Ask death. It is again seized upon by inferior forces, it re-descends and falls back, to recommence its voyage ten, a hundred times, but without ever overstepping the fatal limit. Matter does not produce matter; it travels on in a closed circle. But the soul? Here is seen its sovereignty. The soul rises always, is ever in progress, but never re-descends unless by the free movement of its will. The soul is in perpetual and unlimited progression, carried onwards by a desire which nothing can satisfy or limit. Understand, nothing! The soul describes a trajectory which is a parabola in Infinity.

If you will question yourselves, if you will consult the least of your faculties, whether you be governed by your intellect or your heart, whether you be contemplative by nature or active, whatever you may be, if I adjure you to tell me what you are, you will be forced to admit that there is within you a power, an irresistible force, which nothing can limit. Multiply every ray in this intelligence eager for light, nothing can satisfy it; no Science can close up that gaping abyss, or quench the thirst for knowledge which devours you. After each discovery you will only say, with Newton, "Intelligence is like a child on the sea-shore which seeks to empty the ocean with a shell gathered on its sands; the child can never empty the sea, nor can human intelligence ever exhaust the ocean of truth." We would know everything; it is not enough to say, " Such and such truths are sufficient for me; the domain of experience alone is my province." No, the domain of the knowable for man is all that he has not hitherto explored. When he has exhausted the phenomena, he seeks to know the cause, and when he perceives the secondary causes, he seeks to know the first cause. Eternity will not be too long for him; like a traveller that nothing can stop, he will go forward for ever.

But why do I speak only of intelligence! I would invoke your heart. O you who love, who often love that which is passing more than you should, do you love only the earth? do you love only humanity? If you have known all, if your heart has loved with all the enthusiasm of your twenty years, with all the vigour of maturity, with all the exquisite delicacy of the temperament best formed for affection, if it loves only created beings it will remain empty and unsatisfied. It is useless to tell yourself that the morrow will bring greater and unknown joys that past days have not brought; time brings with it only vanity, every morrow is like the days that have gone before. The one need of the heart, as of the intelligence, is Infinity!

Do not object that man is too ambitious in his aspirations. No, such is his natural impulse. He is in progress of evolution, and must advance; this is his sublime destiny. Who will complain of it?

Everywhere this force declares itself with equal vigour. Follow out man's æsthetic sentiments, the most exalted efforts of his imagination: is his admiration ever surpassed? The masterpieces of art and nature which pass before you, do they ever satiate or even satisfy you? No; your Ideal is higher than all that you behold, and before it the real pales and is imperfect. And this unattained Ideal it is which proves your need for the Infinite and Perfect, and that It is the supreme object of your love, your thought, and your admiration. This is the greatest fact of human consciousness; keep it well before you, for it is the very fibre of my argument. Man is in a perpetual motion, to which it is impossible to assign a term, and which is always superior to every fixed term. A motion to which no term can be assigned is called an indefinite motion. When, in mathematics, you have to do with a quantity which is unknown, and in dynamics with a force whose intensity is not determinable, that force and that number are called an indefinite force, or an indefinite number. What is an indefinite force or number? A force and a number which tend towards something which is greater and higher than every given force and every given number. Now, there are but three things here below: the finite, the infinite, the indefinite. The indefinite is merely the incomprehensible relation between the finite and the infinite. As a real connection supposes the reality of the two terms, when I perceive in finiteness this indefinite movement, I conclude God. Therefore, as we have proved in a palpable manner that intelligence is in progression with an energy that cannot be retained, consequently with an indefinite force; as we have proved that the heart has longings which nothing can control; as we have proved the existence of imaginative powers which nothing can limit—I conclude that Infinity is the term to which all our faculties strive. That great voice which proceeds from our intelligence, our heart, and our imagination is God! You think, O man of Science, that the earth and its mysteries are the limits of your inquiring intellect. No! the limit is Infinity. The highest aim of a loving, beating, insatiable heart is not the love of the creature. That only increases its thirst; the Infinite alone can quench it. And finally, brethren, our highest enthusiasm and admiration is not of this world either; it is not even in that beauty which love surrounds with almost a divine halo. Before the Infinite, towards which we gaze in our greatest moments of spiritual exaltation, all earthly fragile beauty grows dim.

O my God! I pity from my heart those who, in looking into their own souls, have not known or understood Thy presence; those who, calling upon Thy name, have not felt their heart expand, their eyes open to the divine light, and their souls gladdened and refreshed by a breath from the shores of eternity!

Leaving ourselves, let us now listen to the evidence of the human race.

One individual may be deceived: he may mistake his thoughts and aspirations; the testimony of his fellow-creatures is necessary to control his personal doctrines. An individual may be under hallucination, but not an entire race. A man may have insane desires or strange visions; not so an entire species. Let us study history and see from it what humanity thinks of the God I proclaim to you. Observe the mass of mankind; in every age and every country always the same cry, always the same worship. They worship certainly in divers manners, but in spite of all idolatries the One God remains. They bend the knee according to divers rites; God is always the object of devotion. They may blaspheme; it is always God whom they blaspheme. They strive about many things, not always under the same name; it is always God who, under different names, is at the root of every conflict. Humanity has faith in God—it has always had and will always have; the past guarantees the future. But, you will say, "What does such testimony prove? it is based upon number, and number has nothing to do with truth." Indeed, it is so, and I myself have inveighed several times against a majority with regard to truth and justice; why then should I invoke it? Number is not always in the right, nor on the side of truth. I quite agree, when it is alone; but number brings with it some guarantee —for instance, intelligence. If humanity in its numberless mass has confessed God, has intelligent humanity also proclaimed Him? The great geniuses who have passed away, did they confess God, or did they blaspheme Him? Here is the question. Without going back any further than Greece, listen to Pythagoras and Socrates, Aristotle and Plato; and from Rome interrogate Cicero, who embraces all the philosophic eloquence of Rome, and Seneca, the last heathen sage on whose brow shone a ray of evangelical wisdom. Consult all our modern Christian philosophers; the publicity and unanimity of their testimony dispenses me from enumerating these illustrious names. Ancient and modern, pagan and Christian, almost all have immortalized themselves by demonstrating and adoring God. How! is there not an argument against genius? Are number and intelligence infallible? Are they never deceived?

Yes, brethren, they may be deceived; but there is a third guarantee which is absolute. When you see united to number and genius a last element, the most sacred and the most sure—virtue and goodness—my brethren, will you then bow down also? You may rebel against the mass; mankind is liable to aberrations, ignorance, caprice. You may say to genius, "You have conspired against what is true; you have become the accomplice of force; you have listened to the egotistical instincts of your nature: away! I know you not." It might happen that in so doing you would be justified. But that which imposes itself irresistibly, which reveals its healthy nature, that nature which is the very voice of God, is number, genius, and virtue united. When virtue intervenes to prevent genius from listening to the egotism of its dreams, when virtue is there to impose silence upon the low instincts of the mass, how can you do other than acknowledge the authority of virtue sanctioning genius and number? Now, all men of virtue have confessed God; all those who have died in great causes, or have done good to humanity, have been the servants of God, the envoys of Him who put into the heart virtue, which cannot deceive, and which is the prophet of eternity.

Well, my brethren, we belong to the human family in which men of virtue, geniuses, and nations have borne witness to the God whom I announce to you. Let us be with these great representatives of humanity; let us, with them, confess the God of all ages; let us exclaim with this great assembly, "I believe in God!" No, brethren, let us not say, "I believe:" let us say, "I am convinced that the God they proclaim exists! I see Him, I know Him!" When virtue, genius, and number are on our side, truth must be also.

And now let those who are not with us stand apart! Who are you? Show yourselves; what is your number? Do you count, even, in France, in Europe, in the world, in this century which we call the nineteenth, or in all centuries? Will you compare the suffrages? Will you pass in review the army of those who believe only in matter, those who have no altar, and the army of those who bend the knee before God? will you compare the lovely and gentle family of the sons of God, and the mass of those lost children who know Him not?

My brethren, these lost children are of two kinds: there are certain philosophers amongst them, victims of a perverted reason or a pretentious science; and there are the savages who know no longer, or know not yet, how to worship God. Systematic atheists do not fear to proclaim themselves as allies of these degraded offshoots of the human race. They have the weakness to believe the doubtful testimony of travellers, who tell them that certain debased and animalized men do not believe in God, and have no conception of Him, and hence they conclude that God is not natural to the heart of man, because Australians, Bosjesmen, or Caribbees do not name Him! This is their triumphant argument.

Be silent! When the vast and tranquil ocean makes its voice heard, man is dumb. When the rivulet is confounded with the mighty ocean into which it runs, the rivulet has no longer a voice. Those who believe in God are the ocean; those who believe not, this lost stream, whose murmur is imperceptible. Let us be, then, with the mighty ocean, that absorbs in its vastness the little rivulet which would trouble the majesty of its waves!

No, my brethren, it will never be given to any genius, or to any Science, even though the genius be assisted by a whole nation, even though all

Europe should deny the God of its fathers, it will never be given to any one to trouble the harmony of the human family singing the most beautiful of all canticles, and proclaiming God the Father of Nature and humanity, its Beginning, its End, and its Law.

SEVENTH DISCOURSE.

RATIONAL KNOWLEDGE OF GOD.

My Brethren,
 Six centuries ago, in one of those monasteries where Virtue, Science, and Faith together found an asylum, and where the monks received the children of noble families, to train them in the love of God, of study, and of prayer, one of those children, scarcely arrived at the age of reason, put to himself and reiterated to his astonished masters a sublime question. He asked, looking at them with great wondering eyes, "What is God?" "No, but," he repeated, when they had given him some reply, "what *is* God? Tell me, what *is* God?"

That child was Saint Thomas Aquinas; those monks, Benedictines of the thirteenth century. But, my brethren, that child, also, is the human soul; those monks, all that has a voice to reply to its incessant "Why?" all that can satisfy its insatiable and religious curiosity.

Truly, if there is a question which the soul in its thirst for truth asks itself with impatience, a question to which we absolutely require an answer, it is this: What is God? I ask you this to-day, or rather you ask it me yourselves. After we have established that God is, it seems to me that you are asking in your own minds *what* He is. You are Saint Thomas Aquinas, and I represent the monks who endeavoured to answer him.

Is there a possible solution to this problem? Certain sceptics have denied that there is. We will prove to them that they lie. If the solution is possible to the mind of man, whither does it extend, and what are its limits? In short, has the notion of God an actual importance in daily life, or is it only an abstract truth, without influence on the action of things, and on the conduct of free beings? This is the question, my brethren, that we have to examine.

When you have once felt the vital importance of a rational solution of this problem, you will hold it fast. You will no longer permit shameless sophists to attack—in the name of an arrogant Science, or of a reason which they call enfranchised, but which is, on the contrary, enslaved by a thousand prejudices—the one mastering idea which supports all moral life, and to which is attached the fate of nations and the future of humanity.

My brethren, is it possible for human intelligence to answer this question: What is God?

Of course, I consider it an established fact that you cannot escape from this question; it is one which imposes itself upon you, it rises up in spite of yourselves, and it is impossible to silence it. But in that case what an alternative! You must either attempt the herculean task of its solution, or torture yourself in the endeavour to forget it. Questions once raised cannot be put aside; they must either be answered, or remain for ever to vex humanity.

Is it true, then, brethren, that every soul wishes to discover the Divine Nature, and that none can quell within themselves this sublime and pious curiosity?

I hear in the midst of you silent voices saying to me, "No, indeed, such a desire has never entered my head. Nothing troubles me less. I live my life in this world quietly (or anxiously): I am occupied with my business; I see what is useful to me; I go about my house and my little existence; but I assure you I have never asked myself if God exists, nor what He is likely to be."

I acknowledge, my brethren, some souls may act thus and live in this state. But I do affirm that this conduct is affected, and that this state is transitory, and I affirm this without fear of contradiction.

Who has not known it? There are moments when the soul is very far from concerning itself with heavenly things, when it cares nothing for the life beyond this, when earth is all-sufficient for it, and it is absorbed by earthly joys, devoured by earthly anxieties. The soul forgets itself and it forgets God. This is a fact: man has a great faculty for diverting his attention from the Infinite.

But, brethren, this distraction is but short.

However long may be the sleep, day comes at last, and you must open your eyes. However agitated and absorbed you may have been, there comes a time when, in spite of yourself, you are no longer pre-occupied by the affairs of the world that tire you, nor seduced by its pleasures that enervate you, nor carried away by its whirlwind which has cast you aside like a withered leaf; there comes an hour when, against your will, you look beyond, seeking and longing for more than the world can give. Can you escape from this hour? In vain do you call to your aid pleasures that no longer distract you, and turn to this world which shuts its door upon you. Then the Invisible torments you, speaks to your soul, pierces your heart as it were with a poisoned arrow; unsatisfied longings stir your soul; you feel yourself led by an irresistible impulse beyond all created reality, and you say with Descartes in those admirable words, the most poignant and profound in which the secret of consciousness has ever been expressed: "I feel that I am an imperfect and changeable thing, aspiring incessantly towards that which is perfect and unchangeable."

In such an hour—I speak to those who have any imagination—when seated by the vast ocean, whose murmur delight and awes you, or when looking into the stillness of a calm starlight night, into that heaven so much greater than yourself, it is impossible but that, forgetful alike of yourself and your sorrows, you should feel the reality of that mysterious world which none can see, but which alone can fulfil the immensity of our longings!

In your truest nature you touch that unknown of which the sea is an image, and the heavens a figure in their unfathomable profundity—unknowingly, but none the less fervently, your soul cries out to God. Deny it not, or you lie to yourselves.

My brethren, even if imagination is silent, the heart cannot be, and the most hardened hear its voice. When tired, crushed, worn out with anguish, and beaten to the very ground with sorrow and misfortune, like a tree broken down by the tempest, it seems to bend and ask for mercy, does not the human heart in its agony rise to something higher than the earth, and cry aloud for that which it knows and feels this world cannot give? Is there not a supreme moment in which it exclaims, "My God is everything here? Is there not something beyond, since the world cannot satisfy me? O God, is it not Thou that art the all-sufficient One?" Let those who love or have loved, answer. But then we must know who and what this God is; for we cannot love a Being we are ignorant of, and the first want of love is to know the object of its affection. Did the heart not prompt the intelligence, this latter would have but to follow its natural movement to enter that path which leads to the Infinite; and yet, more eagerly than either the heart or the imagination, it will ask itself, What is God? When it has sought for and discovered the law of phenomena, when it is raised by these phenomena from light to light, seeing the end ever fleeing before it, impatient to penetrate the enigma of things, it will also invoke that One who is the origin and end of all, but cannot be grasped in anything visible. You who have loved, have sought for the truth, have dreamt of infinite beauty, is this not your history? It is the history of all that lives and breathes, of all that is intelligent, loving, and imaginative; it is the history of man. What does it mean? It means that in that saddest but most sublime hour of all human life—most sad, because in it we feel our own nothingness; most sublime, because it approaches us nearest to God— we ask ourselves involuntarily, "What is this unknown that ever rises up before us? We see a glimpse of it beyond and above all our dreams, our loves, all that we seek! Always and everywhere it is before us. What, then, is it?" I ask you this question as I ask it to myself. It is momentous and must be solved.

Before any examination, I reply without hesitating, the solution is possible. That these great wants should remain unsatisfied, to be a torture to man, is a repugnant idea. What! not a creature but can satisfy its legitimate instincts, and yet the highest aspiration of man, that which is his divine attribute, which raises him above all else, remains useless, and thus becomes his suffering! No, that is not, that cannot be!

Reason confirms unanswerably this argument taken from the instincts of our great and religious nature. Whenever we perceive an effect, such is the constitution of our intelligence that it can by this effect discover the cause. Now, as we perceive, both in the world and in the soul, numerous effects of the First Cause, we can conclude that our intelligence is capable of knowing God through the world and through the soul. This is the doctrine of Saint Paul: "*The invisible things of God from the creation of the world are clearly seen, being understood by the things that are made.*" What do I say? Not only can God be known, I hasten to add, He *is* known. Humanity knows Him. You all know Him; and truly one would say, when I put this question, that I was speaking to an assemblage of savages, who had never heard the name of this ineffable Being. Why did you not arrest my words? Why did you not say at once, " Enough! The God you preach is living amongst us, in our country, in this Europe, in the whole world; there is not a human being who cannot articulate His name." Can you name that which you do not know! Is there a name more widely known, or one more frequently on the lips, than that of God? Then you have heard and seen Him since you gave Him an appellation? You say, God; the Latins say, Deus; the Greeks, θεος; the Jews, Elohim; the Arabs, Allah. Every nation names Him after their own manner; all, without a single exception, give Him a name. Nor do they stop there; they fear Him and love Him, they pray to Him, and kneeling down they adore Him.

What is praying? Brethren, to pray is to draw near to God. This movement is at times irresistible. If one were an atheist to the very fibre, at certain times, in spite of one's self, the knees would bend and the hands be clasped, or if the knees did not bend, the heart would. The soul expands and escapes—whither? It flies upward and stretches towards the Almighty. Prayer is the movement of the soul stirred by the heart, and carried resistlessly towards the Eternal One.

You pray; therefore you know God. One is not moved by an unknown term. Humanity prays, you all pray: God is no stranger to you. You don't pray daily, nor on Sundays; you are not present at the Christian sacrifice; but, brethren, you pray at your own time. You pray when Death says to you, "On your knees!" you pray when misfortune crushes you in its powerful arms; you pray when despair overwhelms you, when you feel all is lost. In spite of yourself your heart shrinks, and then expands again to give vent to a blessed name; you exclaim, "My God!"

Who is this God? What is His strange and mysterious nature?

You have an innate and confused consciousness; I wish to throw light upon it and define it, and give you an idea of God, which will answer at once to your will and your mind, your want to love and your intelligence.

There are two ways of knowing any one: either to look at their works, or else to ask them who they are, and accept their own testimony.

I wish to know one amongst you. If he is a painter I look at his pictures; a man of action, I consider the results of his activity; a statesman, I study the effects of his policy. In a word, I watch him, and if I wish to gain a more exact idea, I approach him and become admitted to his intimacy, so as to learn and hear from himself his own testimony. "I have followed your actions," I tell him, "I know your talents, I foresee what you may become; but still, what is the mystery of your life? There is always a depth spoken of by no one, a reserve not laid bare by works; initiate me into this secret." And indeed, even if you live for twenty, thirty, forty years, half a century, by the side of a man, you follow him in vain; however little depths he may possess, you cannot penetrate the inmost recesses of his heart. His works reveal to you the exterior of the temple; they do not teach you what is hidden in the sanctuary: they have not revealed to you the secret of his free will, or of that which constitutes the personality, which is, after all, the essence of the human being; into that essence you will not penetrate!

So it is with God. We can learn to know Him in two ways: by His works and by His own evidence.

For the moment I do not wish to appeal to God's own testimony. I will not even inquire if God has revealed Himself such as He is in His inner nature; that is the question of Divine revelation; for the moment I put it aside. I may perhaps be permitted to touch upon it before you some other year, and to introduce you into that world of divine mystery. To-day I pause on the threshold.

By thus limiting ourselves, brethren, our object will be to determine the rational idea of God as it is set forth in His work.

The works of God are the universe and the soul. These are to us God's signature. If we wish to know Him it is to them we must turn. With those two things we cannot know God completely; and thus the notion we can form of Him is necessarily inadequate. "Why?" you will say. "Is not the universe vast and lovely enough? Is there anything to add to the profundity of a space without limit, and to the incommensurable depths of the human soul? If the universe has this immensity, and is displayed in those marvellous beauties that we know; if it is the cosmos, as science calls it— that is to say, splendour—surely it can teach us to know God? What! have not the stars written His name in letters of sufficient brilliancy? Is not the soul of man, with its tumultuous passions, its insatiable heart, its ever-active intelligence, its infinite desires; all the oceans of every world, and the human soul multiplying in perhaps endless humanities—is this not sufficient to reveal God?

No, brethren. Whatever may be the power, the genius, or the ability to translate what you think, what you mean, or what you feel, when you send it forth into the world, if you are a writer, artist, musician, or orator, in short a man who wishes to make his soul sink into the soul of a multitude— I feel it now whilst I am speaking to you—directly you have to work outside yourself, the effect produced is always beneath that which you feel within yourself.

You may invoke every faculty of the intelligence, nothing will do it: the condition is absolute, the law fatal. Every time a sound, be it only a sound, passes your lips to express a sentiment, never does that sound render the fullness of the feeling which absorbs you, never! Not if you put into it all the power of a Talma, never! And the man who says, "I have interpreted my thought," that man condemns himself as but an inferior thinker; and the artist who says, "I have interpreted my dream," will never be a Michel-Angelo or a Raphael. The musician who says, "I have expressed this passion which inspires me," that musician will never, I tell you, be a Mozart or a Beethoven!

Yes, that which is within one, from the moment that it is expressed, falls, through that very reason, into a condition of weakness and insufficiency. And the greatest geniuses, if you study their masterpieces, will give you proof of what I advance.

The finest pages of Bossuet, the most beautiful statues chiselled by Michel-Angelo, are far from being the ideal of these geniuses. Why? Because you have to take into account things outside yourself—matter, marble, the voice, space, time, all fragile and imperfect things. Now, what you feel and think—in a word, the Ideal—is above time, above space, above all realities. It enters into a superior region; and when incarnate in the real it fades.

Well, then, shall I tell you? God does not escape this condition. From the day when the universe was made outside Him it was made imperfect. Having begun it must continue. To continue is to progress towards something that one is not. To progress is to admit imperfection.

Thus we have before us the effects of God, inferior to God. Therefore we cannot through those effects arrive at a complete knowledge of the cause; and that is why our notion of God taken from the universe and the human soul is necessarily imperfect.

So we are limited in the knowledge of God, but yet we would learn what the universe and the human soul can teach us about Him.

I come back to the principle of causality, which will give you the whole secret of such idea of God as human intelligence, outside revelation, can form for itself. Now, this principle is such that there must be absolute relation between the cause and the effect. First of all, whatever is in the effect must exist at least equally in the cause. And if the cause is the absolute First Cause, the Cause which has no cause, as Aristotle said when he called it the *immovable Mover*, then it is not only necessary that what is in the effect should be in the cause, but that which is in the effect must exist in the cause absolutely, without limit, and without imperfection.

That is why we have three ways of enabling us to form an idea of God, starting from the universe and the soul. The first is to ascribe to the cause that which we see in the effect; the second, to ascribe to the cause that which we see in the effect putting aside its imperfections; the third, to ascribe to the cause that which we see in the effect carrying the perfections to infinity. These three ways are called by well-known names: the method of causality, the method of negation or transcendence, and the method of analogy.

By the aid of this triple process, philosophic reason has for ages succeeded in forming for itself a logical notion of God. Seeing all beings proceeding from Him, it called Him the First Cause; seeing all things changed, the Immutable One; seeing the creatures of a day, the Eternal One; seeing worlds scattered in space, the Omnipotent One; seeing all things manifold, imperfect, and infinite, it named Him Unity, Perfection, and Infinitude. The notion of God is that of absolute Being. He IS: this is what everything proclaims, the soul and the universe, the smallest of creatures and the most sublime.

Indeed, if the universe is relative, changing, limited, and partial, you conclude from it Being; but a Being without relation or limit, which depends on no other, but is absolute; for to depend on another is to be in relation to that other. If even the universe did not spread that splendid perspective before our eyes which tempts us to analyze it, if it were no more than vile matter, a grain of sand, an atom, a little dust under your foot, thus reduced it would suffice to raise you by your reason, to God. By asking yourself, Whence comes it? you draw nearer and nearer to the

Absolute, the Being which proceeds from no other and can alone explain every phenomenon.

So that if we know how to follow the spontaneous movement of our intelligent soul, we attain without hindrance to the idea of the Being we seek. The least atom, a blade of grass, a little insect, speaks to us of the Absolute Being; for the smallest molecules, the minutest algæ, the tiniest infusoria, are beings that could never be conceived without Him. Now, when you have Absolute Being you have the true notion of God, that which He Himself declared. Allow me this quotation from revelation, that revelation which is a part of human reason. You come, I said, to the very idea that God Himself gave, already centuries back, to a man who transmitted it through all ages, and which no age has ever mistaken. That man was Moses.

Sent by Jehovah to free his people, Moses said to God, "When I come unto the children of Israel, and shall say unto them, The God of your fathers hath sent me unto you; and they shall say to me, What is His name? what shall I say unto them? And God said unto Moses, I AM THAT I AM: Thus shalt thou say to the children of Israel, I AM hath sent me unto you." You hear: "*I AM*" without restriction. He *is*. Thus there is no limit to His being; He is all activity, power, intelligence, energy, and love.

He is. What words! God speaking to Moses added a most significant speech, and one to which we bear witness unto this day. He said, "This is

My name for ever, and this is My memorial unto all generations."

O Moses, didst thou think when Jehovah spake to thee, that, thousands of years later, a man before a religious assembly should recall that sublime appellation? Didst thou think that he would give to other men, asking the name of God, as thou didst ask it of God Himself, the same answer that thy God and ours gave thee out of the burning bush?

Yes, brethren, I give you that answer. Philosophy interpreted by Pythagoras or Plato himself could not have given a greater. This notion of Absolute Being contains and governs all; all the attributes of God follow with irresistible logic. What are those attributes but the different aspects under which we consider the Absolute Being in relation to ourselves and other creatures, a manner of lisping the name of Jehovah, of spelling out its ineffable letters.

Whatever we say of Him, whether affirmatively or negatively, we always express that He is. We refuse Him certain names, such as change, complexity; but such words imply not-being. We affirm certain qualities in Him, but such qualities are inseparable from being itself. We proclaim God intelligent; but intelligence is the very highest mode of being. We proclaim Him good and loving; but goodness is the perfection of an intelligent being. We acknowledge Him glorious and beautiful; but glory and beauty are the radiation of being.

Would you believe that people wish to take away from this Absolute Being His personality, intelligence, and love? They have dared to say God was impersonal! But if you take away from a being its personality you take away everything. What is there better in it than personality? To be a person is to be an intelligent individuality. And you refuse this to the Infinite? To the infinite of pantheism and materialism if you like: that of matter is impersonality itself; that of pantheism is also impersonal, since it is an abstraction; that of materialistic pantheism is still impersonal, since it is the chaos of matter without form or name. On what grounds would they deprive God of that which is greatest of all? On a false notion of personality. Personality, or intelligent individuality, does not mean limit; it means unity and distinction. An intelligent being is apart and distinct from all that is not himself; that is a personal being. Now, not only do unity and distinction not disagree with the idea of the Infinite, but they become Him more than they do any creature. The Infinite is, or He is not; He transcends all the phenomena of the universe, or He is only an imitation of the Infinite. Infinity is personality itself: a personality of threefold power.

And intelligence and love, how can we take these from that which humanity adores? It is an absurdity and a blasphemy; since indeed, in spite of all, humanity adores and prays to God! Of that God you would make, what? Matter? Of that God you would make, what? A being without intelligence? Brethren, one does not adore matter, or kneel before a thing without intelligence; one loves, adores, and prays to a living Being, a Being with whom one can communicate, a Being that answers you when you say you love Him—a Person, in short. Can one hold commerce with the dust one treads underfoot, with indeterminate beings who do not, properly speaking, exist? And yet humanity holds commerce with God; therefore we must admit in this Being of whom I speak, not only Infinity and perfection, but personality, intelligence, and love.

Then humanity is no longer a miserable dupe, the history of humanity is not a bitter comedy, but we are truly praying, adoring, and loving that One who has the power to receive adoration, prayer, and love, the living God, such as our consciences feel and proclaim Him. For, my brethren, the human conscience, so outraged in this world, must be satisfied at some future time; if not on this sorrowful planet on which justice so often goes astray, at least in other more fortunate worlds, the human conscience must be eased of the vices which scandalize it, and be avenged of the tyrants who have oppressed it. What! You see it struggling with injustice, crushed, laughed at, and it is ever to be a victim? There is to be no just and living Being who shall one day embrace it and give it that freedom for which it cries aloud!

This cannot be, since to all the many attributes we ascribe to God we must add that of justice. Hence we bow before that One who is intelligent, good, powerful, and holy, and who can in His own time make that justice prevail which is to-day too little recognized and so often trodden underfoot.

Do not think that this idea of God is unimportant, that it matters little what is thought about Him, and that it is a simple affair of theory.

Superficial minds, who think themselves practical because they see only the exterior of life, willingly imagine that it is of no consequence whether you think of God after the manner of the materialists or the pantheists, the Jews or the Mahometans, and that the world will go on just the same. We must undeceive them. And to convince them I have but to glance at the chief features of history.

All the individual life of nations and all the moral life of humanity hangs upon the idea of God. And if in studying the philosophy of history you wish to obtain all knowledge of a nation, or of a race and its development, there is only one problem to solve: what idea of God was current in this nation, or in this race, or in this humanity? And in accordance with such an idea so will you have such a nation, such a race, such a civilization, and such a humanity.

That is why, in broaching this question before you, I feel an unspeakable emotion, for we are at a time in which, in France and in Europe, the very idea of God is in question. It is not, believe me, persecution of the Church, nor blasphemy directed against those who represent outwardly the cause of God, that are alone in question; that which is at stake—I tell you with the profoundest conviction—that which is at stake in France, in Europe, and in the whole of humanity, is the idea of God.

You have often heard of the Antichrist: this word has a meaning of its own in Christian literature. By Antichrist is meant that which is opposed to Christ, and it is supposed to contain all that is the worst in humanity given over to evil. Well, there is something even more opposed to Jesus Christ than the Antichrist; that is the Anti-God. It does not only deny Christ, it denies God. It does not only deny the Mediator, it denies Him that sent Him; it does not only deny the glory which shone on the forehead of the Master, it denies the divinity that filled it. It is the negation of God which tends to prevail in this day.

Four ideas of God have in turn ruled mankind. The primitive world awoke as the daybreak of humanity, and the first man felt upon him the breath of his Creator, the touch of the hands that formed him. The idea of a Creator was dominant, and founded the great era of the Patriarchs.

That idea became profaned; everything was worshipped: trees, stones, animals, and men, all were gods. They apotheosized emperors and Cæsars. Paganism reigned.

Nations rose against nation. Egypt fell before Babylon; Persia succumbed to the Medes; the West snatched the sceptre from the East; the armies of Greece penetrated into ancient India. At length Rome arose. She assailed them all; force and oppression reigned. Universal empire prevailed.

The idea of the Godhead became divided. Gods were multiplied. There was strife between them and consequently between the races. The gods of the Capitol prevailed; they subdued the other nations. The gods of Rome cried to the others, "Come near and burn your incense." Beautiful Greece, who multiplied her gods at the will of her genius, brought them all. The East followed the steps of the conqueror; all drew near to the Capitol to burn their incense. They were slaves! From such a notion of God came such a race and such a nation.

And the God of the Jews—the terrible God called Jehovah? He had to be terrible to govern this hard and inconstant people. He had to speak to them through thunder from Sinai, and threaten with death until the fourth generation His guilty worshippers.

He said to Moses, "Go into Egypt and deliver My people; and if they will not let them go I will stretch forth My hand and plague the Egyptians. They will pursue you, but you shall strike with your staff the waves of the Red Sea, and they shall divide, and My people shall go through; but the waters shall come again upon the Egyptians, and they shall be overthrown."

Israel was unfaithful; it set up the golden calf and fell down before this strange divinity. Moses, armed with the power of his mighty God, appeared. He broke the tables of the Law, exclaiming, "The first who bends the knee before the idol shall be struck dead; and serpents shall come among you, whose deadly bite shall testify to the inexorable vengeance of the God whose messenger I am."

And the nation was afraid. Fear is like the salt of the sea; it preserves, and men held by it do not become corrupt. So it was that the terrible Jehovah kept the Jews, and they still live in remembrance of His name of dread.

Then there came a man who had the astonishing power of altering completely the human idea of God. He said, "The God you have till now feared I am come to teach you to love; the God you have known terrible I am come to show you gentle as a father." Then when Jesus appeared in Judea, which still trembled under the implacable scourge of Jehovah, it seemed that the world had taken a leap.

Humanity was changed. After having knelt before its God trembling like a slave, immolated its sons as holocausts, and through fear cast all at His feet, suddenly it awoke; it adored and learned to love the God that a better light revealed to it, and He whom it had only named with trembling is now called Father.

Brethren, you are of that humanity. You love God more than you fear Him. Yes! you love Him, whatever you may say. In spite of yourselves, a profound feeling of love to God stirs in the very depths of your soul. Well, and what is the result of this force? You love God—and then? Then we love one another. Then we say to the slave, "Arise! God has broken your chains." We say to the child helpless in the hands of a cruel father,

" Poor little creature without a refuge against relentless authority! thou hast now a Father in heaven. Fear nothing; thou art adopted by God." Then you say to the wife, " Cast off thy chains, O woman! Thou art the daughter of God, who is the Father of all." Men love one another. Nations call each other brethren. Christian humanity succeeds to pagan; Europe in Christian fraternity to Europe at war; to an enslaved world a world of liberty.

This love has diminished. The idea of God grows dim and becomes effaced. What do I say? Not only have you altered the idea of the Christian God, but you strive to suppress God altogether. Let positivism, materialism, pantheism, the ideas and the lives of sceptics, do their work, and suffer yourselves to be invaded by the vices of this degrading civilization; know that when the idea of God alters, humanity alters. When the idea of God is suppressed, humanity is suppressed. It is destroyed by wars, and by luxury more destructive than wars. When God disappears, races become degraded and humanity extinct. I do not wish to revive the prophecies of Jeremiah, and to exaggerate before your eyes this awful prospect, but you must admit it would be but just to renew the maledictions of the prophets against a humanity that no longer recognizes its Father—which, after having loved, prayed to, and received Him, now blasphemes and will have no more of Him—that exclaims, " Enough! Thou art a burden to me! away, thou God that pursuest me! I want no more either of Thy Christ or Thy divine love. I want my earth, my science, and my own life. I want to belong to myself!"

O you Christians, when you pray to God and raise your hands to Him, ask that the denial of God may not prevail in our land, in our country, and in our age. For, I swear it to you, if the denial of God should prevail, there would be an end of our country, of Europe, and of this planet. The day in which absolute blasphemy shall spring from the desolate heart and the degraded nature of this generation, believe me, the deluge of fire will come, and God the Avenger will open under the feet of this miserable humanity the tomb which will engulf it. Let it not be so. Let us not be still before this melancholy prospect. Let us strive for a better hope. We have a vigorous army of Crusaders to rally round the Cross, and we shall yet see a youth full of hope, which will inflict an utter defeat on all those who wish and think they are able to destroy God.

Fear not. However few there may be who wish to retain Him, God will remain. The idea of God will revive, will spread, and will conquer. If there were but five just men, five just would suffice. They would rekindle faith in God, in His Christ, and in His Church, and thus in that religious faith on which the future and the happiness of our country depends.

Questions that Trouble Beginners in Religion.

By Rev. GEORGE W. SHINN, Newton, Mass.

---

116 pp., 18mo, cloth, 50c.; boards, 25c.

"A very good little manual. It gives simple and practical replies to such questions as relate to faith in a God, in the Scriptures, in a divine Christ, and in supernatural help."—*The Independent.*

"Young men, in all the varied phases of business, would be apt to think favorably if a work of this kind were put into their hands by a friend, an employer, or any one from whom such a gift could not be regarded as an impertinence."—*The Church Standard.*

"All Mr. Shinn's manuals are useful. This will prove more serviceable than any."—*The Iowa Churchman.*

"Very helpful in meeting the ignorance and shallow skepticism so prevalent."—*The Church Eclectic.*

"This little book will be found very interesting, not only for 'beginners in religion,' but for all who are called upon 'to give a reason for the hope there is in them.' It is especially necessary in this day, that all believers should know *why they believe*, for the spirit of the age is decidedly against believing *what* you are told simply *because* you are told. * * * The young have heard of the objections from those not friendly to religion, and have no answer to make because they are taken by surprise. * * * The subjects are treated with fairness; the positions taken are ...oderate and well sustained. * * * The form of the treatis and the cheapness of the volume render it available as a manua for schools and Bible-classes."—*The Living Church.*

THOMAS WHITTAKER, Publisher,

2 & 3 BIBLE HOUSE, NEW YORK

One volume, handsomely printed, 334 pp., 12mo, cloth extra, $1.50.

Modern Heroes of the Mission Field.

By the Rt. Rev. W. PAKENHAM WALSH, D.D., Bishop of Ossary, Ferns and Leighlin. Author of "Heroes of the Mission Field," "The Moabite Stone," etc.

CONTENTS:

I. Henry Martyn: India and Persia, 1805–1812.
II. William Carey: India, 1793–1834.
III. Adoniram Judson: Burmah, 1813–1850.
IV. Robert Morrison: China, 1807–1834.
V. Samuel Marsden: New Zealand, 1814–1838.
VI. John Williams: Polynesia, 1817–1839.
VII. William Johnson: West Africa, 1816–1823.
VIII. John Hunt: Fiji, 1838–1848.
IX. Allen Gardiner: South America, 1835–1851
X. Alexander Duff: India, 1829–1864.
XI. David Livingstone: Africa, 1840–1873.
XII. Bishop Patteson: Melanesia, 1855–1871.

"The American reading world owes a debt of thanks to the publisher for bringing out so good a book in a style of type and paper which leaves nothing to be desired. The book is one which must be read by those who would know its merits. No newspaper notice can do justice to it."—*The Living Church.*

"It is entitled to a place in every library, and should be purchased and read by every one interested in the work of Foreign Missions."—*Gospel in all Lands.*

"A good book to have in hand if one is to keep the divine spirit of the missionary work close to his heart."—*Standard of the Cross.*

THOMAS WHITTAKER, Publisher,
2 & 3 BIBLE HOUSE, NEW YORK.

An Undeveloped Chapter in the Life of Christ.

The great meaning of the word *Metanoia*—lost in the old version, unrecovered in the new. By TREADWELL WALDEN.

8vo, paper, 25 cts. ; cloth, 50 cts.

"Able, excellent, truthful. * * * Has my cordial approval.
"DR. PHILIP SCHAFF."

"I cannot refrain longer to tell you how profoundly important I feel the points you make to be. * * * I am sure that many of our most disastrous failures in commending Christianity to unbelieving minds, especially minds of a manly character, have their cause just here. DR. J. F. GARRISON."

"The essay has very great value. It gives the view of this term which I have long held. DR. MULFORD."

"Scholarly, brilliant, exhaustive. * * * You have done a good service in this elegant and powerful portraiture of the great truth of Christian life.
"DR. H. N. POWERS."

From the REV. PHILLIPS BROOKS, D.D.

"I have just read your 'metanoia' through from beginning to end, and I want to tell you how much I enjoyed it, and how much I thank you for sending it to me. It is full of inspiration. It makes one think of Christian faith as positive and constructive, and not merely destructive and remedial. It makes the work of Christ seem worthy of Christ. I thank you truly, both for writing it and giving it to me. Your sincere friend, PHILLIPS BROOKS."
"BOSTON, Mass."

CHEAP EDITION OF AN ENJOYABLE BOOK.

The Vicar of Morwenstow.

A Life of Robert Stephen Hawker, M.A. By S. BARING-GOULD.

312 pp., 12mo, with portrait. Paper covers, 60c. ; Cloth extra, gilt top, $1.75.

"It is one of the most charming and characteristic biographies which has been written since Isaak Walton sharpened his pen to tell the story of Richard Hooker, George Herbert, and the other worthies of the tempestuous age which preceded him. * * * A book which contains more good stories than any other ecclesiastical biography that has been written within our memory. * * * Every bilious person ought to have a copy. It is a most enjoyable book."—*The Standard of the Cross.*

"All who are fond of original characters and enjoy a hearty laugh, ought to get this biography."—*American Church Review.*

Thomas Whittaker, Publisher, 2 & 3 Bible House, N. Y.

Ecclesia Anglicana.

A History of the Church of Christ in England, from the Earliest to the Present Times. By ARTHUR CHARLES JENNINGS, M.A. With marginal Summaries of paragraphs, and full alphabetical Index.

502 pp., 12mo, cloth, red edges, . . . Price, $2.25.

"At last we have a book on the *whole* history of the Church of England that will be a boon to the professor of ecclesiastical history and a comfort to his students. Put together Bates' College Lectures, Carwithen, Churton, Short, and all the other books through which we used to be obliged to wade in order to acquaint ourselves, tolerably, with the history of our Church, and we should not do more than begin to approach to exact knowledge of its history which Mr. Jennings has furnished us in this single volume. * * * He follows none of the old style types of so-called history, which consists mainly in hero-building. Every man, no matter who, stands or falls, by him, according to his personal worth and actual value in the Church events of his time. Altogether, this work is destined for long use by students of its subject, and we regard its production as one of the noticeable events of the present year."—*The Living Church.*

"An unusually good book."—*The Am. Literary Churchman.*

"One of the most needed and best written historical manuals which has appeared for a long time."—*The Standard of the Cross.*

"The volume is packed with information, given generally in a clear, vivid way."—*The Independent.*

"We know of no general history of the English Church which is as likely to be as serviceable as this, and we are glad to recommend it to our readers."—*The Churchman.*

THOMAS WHITTAKER, Publisher,
Nos. 2 & 3 BIBLE HOUSE, NEW YORK.

ANDREW JUKES' NEW WORK.

The New Man and the Eternal Life.

Notes on the Reiterated Amens of the Son of God. By ANDREW JUKES, author of "Types of Genesis," "The Restitution of all Things," "The Law of the Offerings," "Characteristic Differences of the Four Gospels," etc.

296 pp., 12mo, cloth, . . . *Price, $1.75.*

"'Verily, verily!' Many times did our Lord employ these introductory terms in His discourse. * * * At twelve distinct times does Christ arouse attention to specific doctrines of the kingdom by such reiterations Our author takes up these twelve cases and develops the respective deliverances of the Saviour in the connection. He writes with intense feeling, and with a fullness of Scripture knowledge which seems exceptional. There is much that is stimulating and suggestive, both in the conception of his work and in its execution. * * * The work is a most helpful one, and makes a worthy addition to the list of books already published by this author."—*The Standard*, Chicago.

"Andrew Jukes is a voluminous writer, but he is an original and profound thinker as well. His 'New Man and the Eternal Life' is one of the most original and ingenious of his works, and will have, as it ought to have, a large circulation in this country."—*The Parish Visitor.*

"We have found the book suggestive and spiritually stimulating."—*The Congregationalist.*

"They who want a rich feast may herein eat and be satisfied. 'The New Man' should be read slowly and with concentration; thus every particle will be enjoyed."—*The Living Church.*

"The argument throughout the book is well sustained and intensely interesting. Entirely original, it is a book which will be read and re-read with ever-increasing pleasure and profit."—*The Church Guardian*, Halifax.

THOMAS WHITTAKER, Publisher,
2 & 3 BIBLE HOUSE, NEW YORK.

Studies in the History of the Prayer Book.

[The Anglican Reform. The Puritan Innovations. The Elizabethan Reaction. The Caroline Settlement.] With Appendices.

By HERBERT MORTIMER LUCKOCK, D.D., author of "After Death."

12mo, cloth, uncut edges, ... Price, $1.50.

"The Canon of Ely has already distinguished himself by his book, 'After Death.' In that publication he proved himself the possessor of a fine intellect and a well trained pen. In his new work, entitled 'Studies in the History of the Prayer Book,' he fully maintains the standard of his first treatise. His divisions have a ring about them very like the touch of that master of English history, John Richard Green. The reader feels that in following such a teacher he has at least a living thought as the clue to guide him among the intricacies and technicalities of liturgical study. Dr. Luckock does not seem to have reached the very highest round in the ladder of Anglican Catholicity, but is well up in that direction. He is near enough to Dean Stanley to emulate the realistic touches in 'The History of the Eastern Church,' and at the same time is near enough to Canon Liddon to preserve his clearness of statement on theological points. He has succeeded in clothing some very dry bones with flesh quite rosy and palpitating. The book is thoroughly polished and attractive, and must secure a decided success as the most readable work of its special class."—*The Episcopal Register.*

"It is just the book that every student of the Prayer Book has wanted."—*Standard of the Cross.*

"Liturgical development is becoming a matter of absorbing interest, not only within but without the Church, and the work of Canon Luckock may be regarded as a valuable contribution to the literature of the subject."—*The Churchman.*

Thomas Whittaker, Publisher, 2 & 3 Bible House, N. Y.

New Sermons, full of Thought, gentle Charity, and Spirituality.

Knight-Banneret.

By JOSEPH CROSS, D.D., LL.D.

303 pp., 12mo, cloth, ... *Price, $1.50.*

CONTENTS:

1. JEHOVAH-NISSI.
2. SATAN EVICTED.
3. THE PREACHING OF THE CROSS.
4. THE PRECIOUS VOLUME.
5. ELIJAH, THE TISHBITE.
6. STORMING THE KINGDOM.
7. THE SONGS OF ZION.
8. SANCTIFIED SOLITUDE.
9. CROWN-JEWELS FOR CHRIST.
10. THE DECEITFUL TONGUE.
11. THE TONGUE REFORMED.
12. AN ODIOUS MOUTHFUL.
13. THRONE OF INIQUITY.
14. BATTLE-CALL OF REFORM.
15. WAITING FOR THE LORD.
16. ARMAGEDDON.
17. DAY OF JUDGMENT.
18. FIRST RESURRECTION.
19. MILLENNIAL KINGDOM.
20. ISRAEL'S DESTINY.
21. SIGH FOR THE OLD YEAR.
22. SONG FOR THE NEW YEAR.

The Greatness of Christ,

And other Sermons. By ALEXANDER CRUMMELL, D.D., Rector of St. Luke's (Colored) Church, Washington, D.C.

12mo, cloth, ... *Price, $1.50.*

Extract from the Introduction by Rt. Rev. Thos. Marsh Clark, D.D., LL.D.

"He has ventured to give to the general public this volume, hoping that he may thus reach a larger congregation than could be gathered within sound of his living voice, and also add something to his not over generous income. I think that I may assure the reader that he will find something in these discourses that is fresh and original. The topics considered are varied and interesting, the counsel the preacher gives to his people is sound and practical, and the sermons are pervaded by the life and light and unction of the Gospel."

CONTENTS:

1. THE GREATNESS OF CHRIST.
2. THE FAMILY.
3. MARRIAGE.
4. THE LAMB OF GOD.
5. RISING WITH CHRIST.
6. GLORIFYING GOD.
7. UNBELIEVING NAZARETH.
8. THE REJECTION OF JESUS.
9. THE MOTIVES TO DISCIPLESHIP.
10. THE AGENCIES TO SAINTLY SANCTIFICATION.
11. AFFLUENCE AND RECEPTIVITY.
12. CHRIST RECEIVING AND EATING WITH SINNERS.
13. THE DISCIPLINE OF HUMAN POWERS.
14. JOSEPH.
15. INFLUENCE.
16. BUILDING MEN.
17. CHRISTIAN CONVERSATION.
18. THE SOCIAL PRINCIPLE AMONG A PEOPLE.
19. THE ASSASSINATION OF PRESIDENT GARFIELD.
20. THE DESTINED SUPERIORITY OF THE NEGRO.

THOMAS WHITTAKER, Publisher, Nos. 2 and 3 Bible House, New York.

Character Building.

Talks to Young Men. By Rev. ROBERT S. BARRETT.
16mo, cloth, handsomely stamped in gold and ink, . . Price, 50c.

"The Rev. R. S. Barrett's Talks to Young Men on *Character Building* deserve to be commended. Mr. Barrett is the rector of St. Paul's, Henderson, Ky., and this volume is the report of his unwritten Sunday evening addresses. They are manly, lively, and fruitful off-hand discourses, such as come only from an effective preacher, and make up an excellent volume to be placed in the hands of young men."—*The Independent*.

NEW EDITION OF AN OLD FAVORITE.

The Rector of St. Bardolph's;

Or, Superannuated. By FREDERICK W. SHELTON, D.D., author of "Salander and the Dragon," "Peeps from a Belfry," etc.
344 pp., 12mo, cloth extra, price, $1.25.

"It is many years since this book, now re-issued, first appeared. In the past it has accomplished not only an interesting but also a very useful task, and, for the long future, we trust it is destined to continue its mission of good-humored instruction on the relations of pastor and people. To the younger clergy, who may expect to meet just such 'snags,' and would know how to steer the sensitive bark of their personal ministry safe around and by them, we would commend a quiet evening by this winter's fireside, with 'The Rector of St. Bardolph's' in their hands, as a friendly chart and sensible guide. Equally we recommend all those who have their eyes upon other folks that *are* 'cantankerous,' to get the book, and deal out to them gathered counsels from its pages."—*The Living Church*.

THIRTEENTH EDITION.

Short Sermons

For Families and Destitute Parishes. By JOHN N. NORTON, D.D., author of "Every Sunday," "Golden Truths," "Warning and Teaching," "Old Paths," "The King's Ferry-boat," etc., etc.
487 pp., 8vo, cloth, price, $2.00.

"The late Dr. Norton * * * had remarkable ability to interest plain people, and this collection of sermons for families and destitute parishes holds its place among the volumes of sermons useful for lay reading chiefly on the ground of the author's art of putting things. The Sermons cover a wide range, and are so interesting that one likes to read them again and again. They are probably the best of their kind."—*The Standard of the Cross*.

"This new issue is proof enough of the popularity and adaptedness for the purpose expressed."—*The Church Eclectic*.

The BISHOP OF MISSOURI says: "I have frequently, in public and in private, recommended Dr. Norton's books."

The BISHOP OF NEW JERSEY says: "I always recommend them."

THOMAS WHITTAKER, PUBLISHER, 2 & 3 BIBLE HOUSE, NEW YORK.

www.ingramcontent.com/pod-product-compliance
Lightning Source LLC
Chambersburg PA
CBHW021808230426
43669CB00008B/678